Just Sayin'

MY LIFE IN WORDS

Malorie Blackman

Just Sayin'

MY LIFE IN WORDS

1 3 5 7 9 10 8 6 4 2

#Merky Books
20 Vauxhall Bridge Road
London SW1V 2SA

#Merky Books is part of the Penguin Random House group of companies
whose addresses can be found at global.penguinrandomhouse.com.

Penguin
Random House
UK

First published by #Merky Books in 2022.

www.penguin.co.uk

A CIP catalogue record for this book is available from the British Library.

ISBN 9781529118674 (hardback)
ISBN 9781529118681 (trade paperback)

Typeset in 12/14.75pt Dante MT Std by Jouve (UK), Milton Keynes.
Printed and bound in Great Britain by Clays Ltd, Elcograf S.p.A.

The authorised representative in the EEA is Penguin Random House Ireland,
Morrison Chambers, 32 Nassau Street, Dublin D02 YH68.

www.greenpenguin.co.uk

Penguin Random House is committed to a sustainable future
for our business, our readers and our planet. This book is made
from Forest Stewardship Council® certified paper.

This book is dedicated to Neil and Liz.
Love you.

And for Chris, who I never got to meet.
And for Tara, who I did meet, but all too briefly.

Perfer et obdura, dolor hic tibi proderit olim.
Be patient and tough; someday this pain will be useful to you.

– Ovid

Not everyone who chased the zebra caught it,
but she who caught it, chased it.

– African proverb

Contents

Foreword	1
Wonder	7
Loss	49
Anger	127
Perseverance	173
Representation	225
Love	245
Acknowledgements	273

Foreword

When I was asked if I'd be interested in writing a memoir, I blithely said yes, thinking, 'How hard can it be to write about yourself?' I'd written over seventy books, instigated events that I'm proud of, done a few things that I'm less proud of, and was ready – or so I thought – to write about them all. It was suggested that I make this book a memoir highlighting the major incidents in my life and their influence on my writing.

Easy?

Not quite.

When I finally sat down to write about my past, I quickly found out I'd got it wrong. Very wrong. This book is the hardest thing I've ever written. Dredging up the painful events of long ago was incredibly difficult. I thought the past would lend an emotional distance to the recounting of various events. Not so. Writing about those events meant living through them all over again as if I were back in that moment.

In my novels, I could imagine the lives, thoughts and feelings of my characters by empathising with them and walking in their shoes for a while, but then I could take off those shoes. I had to let go of my characters to be able to move on to the next story I wanted to write. In novels such as *Pig-Heart Boy*, the *Noughts and Crosses* series and *Boys Don't Cry*, I wrote about real trauma and real emotions, revealing and exploring them within the lives of my fictional characters. I could walk, run, dance or crawl with my characters to hell and back and feel connected to them, in tune with them, but know that they weren't real and were under the control of my pen or keyboard. But writing this book, writing my life story, left me with nowhere to hide and I had to face up to and interrogate certain events and the buried or abandoned traumas from the past. I could identify certain moments as those that made me the person I am and provided the reason I write. 'Why am I an author?' became the question I wanted to examine more deeply, and that investigation is what I'm sharing in these pages.

The simple answer is because somewhere between my brain and my mouth, the words sometimes falter and fall and fail. But somewhere between my brain and my fingers, the words falter, fall and fail less often. Writing became a way to not just organise my thoughts and feelings but to view them with more objectivity and understanding. Writing also became a safety valve – a secret, less judgemental way to address and express myself.

When I was a teenager and life was so close to unbearable that I could barely stand up, never mind stand straight, I'd turn to words and write poetry to pour out my hidden thoughts and feelings. I'd write until it became second nature, and the page became my sanctuary. To my surprise that instinct came back to me writing this memoir. Accessing the incidents of my past and trying to write about them in a relatively objective yet heartfelt manner was difficult, until I faced the most traumatic moments of my life and wrote them in verse. Free-form verse. Most of my story is told in prose but some moments are told as narrative verse. For those not into poetry, I hope that doesn't put you off, but poetry and writing poetry has always been an excellent way of getting to the heart and soul of a matter without prevarication, shame or self-delusion.

This book is a skip and a trip through my years, but not in chronological order. Instead, it has been ordered around some of the major facets of my life, with anecdotes, incidents and accidents highlighting them.

There are songs and poems I love that not only speak to me but wrap their arms around me: for example, the songs from Marvin Gaye's masterful album *What's Going On*, or Stevie Wonder's genius album *Songs in the Key of Life*; the song 'Believer' by Imagine Dragons might've been written just for me, the works of Shakespeare, Benjamin Zephaniah, Maya Angelou, Wendy Cope, Milton. These stories, songs and poems have all reassured me that I'm not alone in the way I think and feel.

Finding the right form for this autobiography wasn't the only unexpected difficulty. Seeing my past on the page forced me to examine some aspects of my life and, more importantly, those people whose words and deeds had an influence on my thoughts and actions, in both a negative and a positive way. Regarding the ones who have had an affirming effect on me, their influence hasn't necessarily been constant, but it's there, and in some way I see my writing as a homage to them too. So, I directed my memories and musings to three very special people and, when I did, it became easier to express my thoughts and write these words. This book is for all my children – Liz (who knows my story already), Chris (who I never got to meet) and Tara. Especially Tara, who, when she was no bigger than the palm of my hand, was taken from me.

Our childhood years are both formative and informative. They're painful, they're confusing, they're joyful and filled with laughter and tears. I've always thought that part of what I do as an author is to connect with not just other children, but the child within myself. To root that child in a safer and stronger place. By focusing on the possibilities of imagination, stories help us to prepare for the future – so that when we become adults we can look back and access our memories for better, or perhaps worse, and note with confidence how they shaped the person we are today. This is the very premise I explored in my book *Thief!*, where the protagonist Lydia wakes up forty years in the future and meets herself as an adult, hating what she has become. We make promises to our young selves to do better, to be better. Sometimes we succeed, sometimes we fail, but the truth is our childhood years matter.

One of my favourite *Star Trek: The Next Generation* episodes is called 'Tapestry'. In it Captain Jean-Luc Picard (played by the sublime Sir Patrick Stewart) dies, only to wake up again in a realm between life and death. He's been shot with a weapon that has destroyed his artificial heart – the implanted organ that has kept him alive since losing his natural heart in a bar brawl as a young man. Picard has always regretted this incident, despite it setting him on the straight and narrow. He's given the chance to go back and set that night 'right', correcting a decision that has plagued him since his youth. However, doing so completely changes his future. He doesn't rise to be captain of the Starship Enterprise, but is a lowly ensign committed to doing routine work, 'bereft of passion and imagination'. He sees that the regrettable incident taught him something. It gave him a sense of morality, drive and purpose. He knew that life was too precious to waste by being cautious and safe. That incident was a catalyst and spurred him on to become the person and the captain he was. After this revelation, he declares, 'I would rather die as the man I was than live the life I just saw.' He's transported back in time once again and doesn't change a thing about the bar brawl. He dies smiling, before being whisked away to get his artificial heart fitted.

The truth is, none of us get to see what other paths or lives might exist for us if we made different choices. But as an author

I get to imagine; I get to create and explore alternative paths or worlds and let my characters live in those spaces and places. As an author, I get to speculate.

Writing this book made me look more closely at the most painful and traumatic moments in my life. I suspect that, without them, I would still be trapped in a career that I found totally unfulfilling. But looking through a microscope on the darkest and lightest moments has also filled me with a sense of hope, not just about my life, but about how my words might encourage others. Writing has given me the chance to communicate and connect with my readers and I want to urge others, no matter their background or the walk of life, to write their own stories, embrace their own truth and own it.

There is still a perception that you must have deep pockets and/or dance with unicorns across rainbow bridges to become an author. That simply isn't true. My life has given me myriad stories, as you're going to see. It's also hopefully given me some insight. There's very little in my past that I would change, perhaps none of it, because my past has made me the person I am today, the writer I am today. This book is me owning that. This is the story of my life, my thoughts and feelings, my joys, my fears. It's not a 'how to live better' book. Ha! I'm *still* trying to figure that one out.

This is just my story, plain and simple.

With love.

Wonder

I

Dear Tara,

I wasn't going to start this at the beginning. Everyone starts at the beginning, and I like to be different, but different in a logical way. The thing is, it took time to realise that my version of logic doesn't run along the well-worn track of most other people's.

I mean, that's the kind of child I was. Things that made no logical sense were challenged immediately. It didn't endear me to friends, acquaintances, classmates or teachers.

My logic was served
*   With a side order of pedantic*
*   Glazed with an argumentative, tart drizzle.*

It took a while to realise that none of my friends thought or acted with the same compulsion as I did. I was laughed at, ridiculed and considered very strange. So, I learned to hide my true self. Sometimes even from myself.

Growing up I was too literal, too gullible, which made school tough to navigate. It also made family and friends tricky to negotiate. Taking people at their word, seeing the world differently from others – always fifteen degrees out, or fifteen minutes ahead, or fifteen minutes behind – was tiring. I hellishly nit-picked every little statement that I believed to be incorrect. This was me trying to grasp for truth and meaning, and to reassure myself that I had got a fact or a situation right. For everyone else it was damned annoying, and I knew it, but I couldn't help it. Blaming myself, blaming my brain for being alternatively wired, was an almost everyday occurrence. It's a facet of myself that took me too long, far too long, to embrace, cherish and, more importantly, value.

Back to where to start. Sometimes, when telling a story, being different just for the sake of it is its own cliché. So here are the foundations on which the bricks of my life have been laid. I was born to Ruby and Joe on 8 February 1962 at Nelson's Hospital, Merton in Surrey. Mum and Dad lived in Clapham at the time. My mum and dad came to Britain from Barbados at the invitation of the then-government to do the jobs that white people didn't want to do. My dad was a master craftsman carpenter, but he drove buses when he arrived in Britain. My mum worked in a factory as a machinist, making pyjamas, soft furnishings and stuffed toys.

When I was a teen, Mum told me that she'd had to leave school when she was fourteen to be apprenticed to a seamstress and earn a living. She'd been desperate to stay on at school but, as it had to be paid for past the age of fourteen, that luxury was reserved for the boys in her family. My parents' plan was to come to Britain and carve out a better future for themselves and all their children.

The first house I remember living in was the one we moved to when I was four years old. It was a three-up, two-down house on Birkbeck Road in the London suburb of Beckenham. When we first moved in, there was just Mum, Dad and my two younger brothers, James and John. Then Mum and Dad told me I had an older sister, Wendy, and an older brother, Vincent, who were born in Barbados and who were still living with my nan over there.

I couldn't believe it. I had an older sister and brother. I couldn't stop talking about them, thinking about them. I was desperate to meet them and Mum was determined that we'd all be together. As soon as they could, my mum and dad sent for my older siblings to join us in England. We went to pick them up at Heathrow and I was so excited. On the journey back, I told them all about their bedrooms and everything we'd done to get them ready – repainting the rooms, new beds, a new wardrobe. I had an extra sister and brother and it was going to be wonderful. Wendy told me years later that I babbled on and on nonstop all the way home from Heathrow and she couldn't understand a word I was saying because my English accent was impenetrable!

In our house the back room, as we called it, contained an upright piano. I can't remember anything else about that room but plink-plonking on the piano. I remember my childhood as one spent playing in the garden, picking pears from the tree, going to the park, going to school. It was a normal, average, everyday childhood for the most part. What I particularly remember was that our house was filled with music. We had an old-fashioned gramophone and my parents played the grooves out of classic Motown albums by groups like the Supremes and the Temptations, as well as Fats Domino's *Greatest Hits* and records by the Mighty Sparrow – a calypso legend from Barbados. Plus, Mum always had on the radio – Radio Caroline mostly. That's where my love of music came from. I was immersed in it, baptised by blues, soul, reggae and pop. I made a point of learning the words to the songs I loved. After one or two listens I would have most, if not all, of the lyrics memorised. And I was constantly singing, though I couldn't and still can't carry a tune in a bucket. One of my favourites was 'A Lover's Concerto' by the Toys (written and produced by Sandy Linzer and Denny Randell). I loved the song so much and it was only later that I learned about the tune's nod to Christian Petzold's 'Minuet in G Minor'. I also enjoyed a number of Beatles songs, like 'Ob-La-Di, Ob-La-Da' and 'Paperback Writer'.

Just as quickly as I could learn the lyrics of songs, I would memorise all the nursery rhymes I enjoyed, and from nursery rhymes grew a love of poetry. I liked the funny ones, like some of the poems from Lewis Carroll's *Alice in Wonderland*, Hilaire Belloc's 'Matilda' and Edward Lear's 'The Pobble Who Has No Toes'. I liked silly as well as serious poems and songs. That's why, when I was invited to be a guest on BBC Radio 4's *Desert Island Discs*, one of the songs I chose was 'Right Said Fred' by Bernard Cribbins, which used to make me laugh every time it came on the radio.

That song along with many others became vessels for happy memories. And there's something to be said for learning songs by heart. I'm sure it helped later with the ability to memorise longer poems, quotes from stories and plays, facts from science, figures and dates in history and the arts and mathematical formulae.

But even nursery rhymes weren't safe from my relentless habit of interrogation. The eighteenth-century nursery rhyme 'Who Killed Cock Robin?' fascinated and frustrated me in equal measure. It gives us the who, the where, the weapon used to kill Cock Robin. We get the witness statements and the funeral arrangements, but we never get the *why*. When I was older, I would read all kinds of theories about it; some sources stated that the poem was about Robin Hood, others said it was about Sir Robert Walpole, an early (some say the first) prime minister of Britain. But as a child, I was left with unanswered questions, which annoyed the hell out of me.

Of all the questions – what, where, when, who, why and how – 'why' is the one I ask most often. 'Why' is the one that interests me the most. Whatever the medium – fiction, song or poem – I like to know why the characters act the way they do. What drives them? Motivates them? What are their ambitions and objectives? What's going on in their heads? What led them to behave in certain ways? Those questions are all variations of 'why'. And I'm sure it's that question I attempt to answer in most, if not all, of my novels.

One of my earliest childhood memories is from my third birthday. Our front room had an open fire, which Mum would clean out every day. I remember watching her light the fire – coals, bits of wood and torn-up strips of newspaper all built up like a layered incendiary cake. It was a typical February afternoon, cold and crisp outside, so the fire in the front room was blazing. Dad came home from work carrying a huge box just for me.

'Happy birthday, sweetheart.' Dad beamed and proceeded to take out a doll almost as tall as me from the box.

The doll was white with nutmeg-coloured hair that reached past her shoulders and open, staring eyes. Cold eyes. Soulless eyes. Dad stood her on her feet and pulled a cord attached to her back. Her arms outstretched, the doll started walking towards me.

'Mama . . . Mama . . .' Its voice was as soulless as its eyes. I watched in horror. 'Mama . . .'

It kept coming towards me. I screamed, picked up the doll and chucked it straight in the fire. Then I burst into tears, staring at Dad, wondering why he would give me such a nasty, creepy thing for my birthday. Dad stared back at me, his expression incredulous. Then he cracked up laughing – which made my tears flow faster. Now, that doll wasn't cheap. I count myself lucky that he was in a good mood or the outcome might've been very different. Instead of shouting at me for the waste of his money, he picked me up and gave me a hug, and all the time laughing. I was never a huge fan of dolls after that.

I have another memory from later that same year, 1965. I'm in a hospital ward full of cots, crying my eyes out. I had the measles and, as my brothers James and John had only just been born, I couldn't stay in the house; I was highly infectious and a danger to them. So there I was, stuck in a hospital ward with other toddlers, wondering *why*. I felt abandoned, unwanted and utterly miserable. My parents came to visit me on the ward and, years later, they each had their own version of events.

Mum said, 'The nurses told us you cried and cried and wouldn't stop. You kept saying, "I want my mummy. I want my mummy!"' Mum smiled indulgently when she told me that story.

Dad said, 'The nurses told us you cried your eyes out. Nothing they did would make you stop. And you kept saying, "I want my daddy. I want my daddy!"' Dad smiled with satisfaction when he told me that.

To this day I remember being in a children's ward at the hospital with rows and rows of cots, but I don't remember which of my parents I used to cry out for. The experience left its mark, though. I'm sure my need to do for myself, fend for myself and rely on no one stemmed from that moment, only to be reinforced as I grew older.

When I was a very young child, my dad used to mock the way I spoke if I spoke Bajan.

'Speak proper English,' he would say. 'The only way you'll get anywhere in this country is if you speak proper English.'

Britain was the mother country and he insisted we had to

assimilate. Our own cultural heritage was deemed less important. When I was a teen, Mum told me that all the books she
had read at school in Barbados – fiction and non-fiction – were
by and about white people. Even in a country with a majority
Black population, Black people were not represented in the literature taught in schools. No wonder, then, that my dad's attitude to his own heritage took the shape it did.

I once said in front of Dad that I was packing my grip to go
on a trip. A 'grip' is what people from many West Indian countries called their travel bag or suitcase. It was a well-known term
in our community. When he heard me say this, my dad grabbed
my upper arm and squeezed hard.

'That's a grip,' he told me in no uncertain terms, squeezing
harder. 'What you want to pack is a suitcase.' Then he let go.

I never called it a grip again.

If I spoke with a Bajan accent, Dad would get angry. If I used
Bajan idioms, he'd get annoyed. This happened repeatedly until
I lost any kind of heritage accent. Permanently. I'm sad to say
that even though I can recognise one at twenty paces, I can't
hold a conversation using a Bajan accent. While I understand
my dad's reasons, I feel sad that part of my heritage has been
denied me. Mum didn't argue because she too believed it was
the best way to survive in Britain. All requests for stories from
and about Barbados were waved aside by both my parents. In
my late twenties, I had to first nag then beg my mum before
she'd open up about her childhood. Some of her stories I incorp-
orated into my *Betsey Biggalow* series of books – with her permission of course! But stories of her childhood were few and
far between, dismissed as irrelevant.

I know it was done for the best of intentions, but it feels like
a part of me has been lost for good. My dad used to say that as a
Black person in the UK, I'd have to work twice as hard and know

twice as much to get half as far. Correcting how I spoke was his attempt to make sure I would fit into British society – in a way that he and my mum would never be allowed to. While Mum didn't agree with his methods, I think she did agree with his philosophy. Mum wanted all her children to thrive in Britain. That's why Mum and Dad had moved here in the first place, after all: so that their children could have a decent education, maybe go on to university and get a good job at the end of it. They felt we'd have more opportunities, more doors opened to us in Britain. It's the same for so many people from an immigrant background or immigrant heritage. There's an innate sense that no one is going to give us anything so we must work hard and expend blood, sweat and tears to set foot on life's ladder.

When it comes to writing, I've always encouraged adults and children alike to cultivate their own voices. To not be afraid or ashamed to use their own style of speaking, their own culture's idioms and ways of expressing themselves. It's these differences that add richness and texture to writing. It's these differences that add richness and texture to life.

From 2013 until it ended, I was one of the judges of the BBC's 500 Words competition, set up by DJ and presenter Chris Evans. The competition invited children aged five to thirteen from across the UK to submit their stories of no more than 500 words. It never ceased to amaze me how much variety and depth those young writers showed in their work. The competition was split into two age categories – five to nine, and ten to thirteen. We judges – Chris Evans, the writers Francesca Simon, Frank Cottrell-Boyce and Charlie Higson, as well as HRH The Duchess of Cornwall – would assemble for a morning at a BBC meeting room and whittle down the entries to a bronze, silver and gold winner in each age category.

Reading through the final fifty story entries was always one of the highlights of my year. However, as part of the selection process, each judge was expected to read out loud at least one of the shortlisted six or seven to help us narrow them down to the final three. I *hated* that bit. It was instilled in me when I was young that my reading voice was 'too common', 'too working class'. When I was at secondary school, our English language O-level exam had a speaking component where we had to read from a passage in a book and then discuss it. I worked hard to improve my diction to pass the exam. I enunciated my vowels, rounded my tones . . . I spoke as if I had a mouth full of marbles, until I grew to hate reading out loud. The whole process made me incredibly self-conscious and still affects the way I read out loud as an adult. I'm no good at it unless I'm reading to children, where I can be myself. Reading to adults makes me nervous, and I tend to just get through the words on the page rather than trying to convey any emotion or meaning. When I read to children, they're listening to the story. They're not interested in my accent, how I pronounce certain words, whether or not I pronounce the 't' in often – as long as they understand what I'm saying. It's something I caution teachers and parents about to this day – don't mock the way your students and children speak because it ruins their confidence in their own abilities.

Different ways of speaking, of looking, of acting are themes I embrace in a number of my books, including *Cloud Busting* and *Chasing the Stars*. I also once wrote a book called *Rachel and the Difference Thief* (long out of print), where a thief stole all the differences in a kingdom, until everyone looked, sounded and acted the same – and what a dull, mundane place it was!

The differences between us apply spice and wonder to life. Just sayin'.

2

Perhaps it was lack of volunteered stories about my parents' childhoods that made me want to fill that void. The only time I remember my parents reminiscing was when relatives or friends from Barbados came to visit. Then I'd sit on the floor doing jigsaw puzzles or filling up my colouring books and avidly listen to the conversations flowing around me. They spoke of people I didn't know, places I hadn't seen, sights, sounds and smells I couldn't recognise, but I stored the information like a squirrel hoarding nuts for winter. I found that if I stayed quiet, the conversation would continue as if I wasn't there and I'd learn far more than if I asked for details or clarification on some of the juicier stories going on around me – like whose wife had run away with someone else's husband when they were both middle-aged and deemed old enough to know better, or which person had died after being knocked off his bike and the effect his death had on his family. Even though I'd never met these people, I knew about them. I knew their stories and that brought me closer to them and their lives. I cherished that.

When I was seven or eight, Mum took me to the dentist to have a tooth extracted. I'd been having excruciating toothache for a while – one of my molars was paying the price of too many strawberry sherbets. The dentist was situated on the second floor of a health clinic building on Penge High Street. A doctor's surgery occupied the first floor. Having never been to the dentist before, I was all eyes and ears as I took in my surroundings – single chairs pushed against the walls, the sweet smell of antiseptic, women's magazines on a dark wood coffee table in the centre of the waiting room. That's the way I was with all new places I visited. I'd drink them in, letting each of my senses take over in turn to experience the situation to the fullest.

A tall dentist with toffee-brown hair came out of a side room and explained to Mum that I'd have gas to knock me out, he'd extract the rotten tooth and, when I woke up, I could go home. So I was led into the dentist's room and sat down on an elongated chair that could be raised and lowered with the depression of a foot lever. A rubber mask was placed over my face, and I was told to count backwards from one hundred. I think I reached ninety-seven, then complete darkness.

But only momentarily.

Instantly I felt warm and safe. Totally serene. My body was floating slowly up and up into the sky, which was a deep blue and dotted with clouds, just like on a perfect summer's day. *The* perfect summer's day. I wasn't flying, just floating. Higher and higher. It was peaceful and something more: blissful. I looked around and there was no one else in sight but I didn't feel alone. I felt loved and cherished – and happy. Truly happy. I wanted nothing more than to keep floating. The higher I got, the happier I grew. Until I was pulled back down very fast by some unknown force and everything went dark. When I opened my eyes again, I was back in the dentist's chair with the tall dentist and another, shorter man with sandy brown hair and matching eyes staring at me anxiously. Behind them was the receptionist from the waiting room, her eyes wide with fright.

'Oh my God. Are you all right?' asked the man I'd never seen before.

'Who are you?' I asked.

'I'm a doctor from the floor below,' he replied. 'Your heart stopped. How are you feeling?'

I smiled at him. 'I feel fine.' And I really did.

Better than fine. I felt great. The best I'd ever felt. The only negative emotion I felt in that moment was regret that they had woken me up. The dentist insisted that I stay in the waiting room with my mum for at least an hour before going home. I sat watching others come and go, puzzled by all the fuss. A girl who went in to see the dentist after me came out fifteen minutes later bawling her head off. 'Why is she crying?' I wondered. Being at the dentist was an amazing experience.

'Mum, when can I come back again?' I asked. 'I want to come here again.'

I'm not even sure if they told my mum what had happened to me; she seemed as confused as I was about why we'd had to wait so long before leaving. I guess the receptionist was made to run for the doctor and I had no idea how he revived me, but he did. For some reason I can't explain, I never spoke to Mum about the experience either.

Now, here's the thing. Thinking about that day afterwards made me wonder – *what if?* Did parallel worlds exist? A unified multiverse? Was there another world where the doctor got to me too late, and was unable to bring me back? A parallel world where my heart had stopped and I died in the dentist's chair? Maybe that was the start of my fascination with the multiverse. 'What if?' became a favourite phrase. Considering 'what if?' scenarios became a favourite pastime.

I wondered about my mum and dad in that parallel world where I didn't make it out of the dentist's chair. In that world, did they stay together or did they separate because they couldn't find a way to comfort each other? I wondered how long till they stopped grieving and remembered me with a smile. Do I believe that we are not alone in the universe and that life exists on other planets? Of course I do. Do I believe in the multiverse? Parallel worlds where every choice we've declined in this world gets to play out elsewhere? I'm open to the possibility. As Hamlet says, 'There are more things in heaven and Earth, Horatio, than are dreamt of in your philosophy.' If I were standing next to Horatio in that moment, my reply would be, 'I genuinely hope so.'

My love of reading had started to develop by the time I was four or five. The characters I read in good books – their lives seemed so vivid to me. The characters I met in great books – they were real long past the point I'd finished reading about them. A real world existed within the pages of each and every good book I read. It made me wonder if those characters truly existed, but in a reality other than my own. If so, were those characters oblivious to the fact their lives were confined to the pages of a book, contained between a front and back cover? What if the world I thought I knew only existed between the covers of a book in some great cosmic library somewhere? Would that make any difference to the way I lived my life? What if the whole of existence was merely a set of nested realities? Even the act of reading fascinated me. The way that shapes and symbols on a page had an ascribed meaning that could be accessed if you were lucky enough to be able to decipher them.

I loved stories with characters so real that I didn't doubt for a moment their lives continued beyond observation. Stories that left a thread or two untied to allow room for the reader to tie up the tale in their own way were my favourite. I continued the stories of favourite characters once I'd finished reading about them, trying to answer the question, 'What happens next?'

What happened to Jill Pole in C. S. Lewis's *The Silver Chair* after she returned from Narnia? How did the experience change her? Did facing her greatest fear make her a stronger person? A better person?

What happened to the second Mrs de Winter in Daphne du Maurier's *Rebecca* when she learned exactly how her husband Max had been involved in his first wife's disappearance? Did the knowledge give her confidence? Did it change her view of her husband?

I believe this set a pattern for the types of endings I wanted to write for my own novels. Speculating about the future lives of characters I met in books made me want readers of my novels to have the same experience. I came back to this philosophy when I wrote one of the final chapters of *Endgame*, in which one of my characters is dying. She is euphoric at seeing a long-lost loved one. Without divulging too many details (spoilers!), this character doesn't know if she's having one last daydream, or if, having discovered the afterlife, she's seeing a loved one who passed years before. This character decides it doesn't matter, because she can live an eternity in that one precious moment of love and reconciliation. *Endgame* also concludes with a protagonist swearing revenge on another main character. It's then left up to the reader to decide whether they will go through with it.

Wondering about the lives of the characters I read in stories made me wonder about the lives of the real people I passed in the street or saw on the TV. What were their likes, their loves, their fears, their ambitions? What did they want most? Did they already have it? Did they have hidden powers? Secret dreams? Were they good or evil? I became a people watcher.

It's a habit I never grew out of.

3

When I was five or six, Mum took me on my first trip to the local public library. I don't remember much about the journey, except that we passed more houses than shops. We walked into the building hand in hand and turned right into the children's library. Once inside, I stopped abruptly and looked around in wonder.

Shelf after shelf, bookcase after bookcase filled with books. And they were all waiting to be read. By me. I couldn't believe I could borrow any book I wanted free of charge. It was amazing. Nothing short of miraculous. I gathered a few books with bright, interesting covers, including *Mr Meddle's Muddles* by Enid Blyton and *Green Eggs and Ham* by Dr Seuss. The cardboard tickets within the books were removed and put in the cardboard wallet that had my name and address on it, which was then filed by the librarian. And the books were mine – even if only temporarily. I hugged them to me all the way home, immediately disappeared into the bedroom I shared with my sister, and I started to read. I can't remember a time when I didn't love stories, but having them written down gave them a permanence, a tangibility, that I relished. I pored over the words, I dived into the illustrations, I didn't just read with my eyes but all my senses.

I entered the world of books, never wanting to leave.

I read the library books over and over, thrilled at getting to select the stories for myself and enjoy them by myself. I particularly enjoyed *Green Eggs and Ham,* loving the rhyme, the humour and quirky illustrations of creatures I'd never seen before. The following week, I swapped them for more Dr Seuss books and Enid Blyton's *Mr Meddle's Mischief*. OK, I thought, so this wasn't a jest or an April Fool's joke. Every book in the children's library was mine to read if I wanted. And I did want – very much. With grateful joy, I made a vow to read every single one of them.

Now, most of the time I got on with my brothers and sisters. Sometimes I didn't. But it didn't take long to realise that my older sister Wendy and my older brother Vincent had each other and a whole history in Barbados that I knew nothing about. My younger brothers were twins and had each other. I was a middle child and, though we all often played together, there were times when I felt like the odd one out. There were times when I was alone, even though our home was full. Usually I didn't mind. Occasionally I did. During those times, books were my friends, my extended family. That's partly why I cherished them. Favourite books like the fairy-tale collections of Andrew Lang and Ruth Manning-Sanders were borrowed and brought home often so that they, like true friends, were always there if I needed them.

Libraries made me hope, work and plan for better times. The books they contained presented me with alternatives. Alternative ways of thinking, of being. They also showed me what I was missing. They made me believe that if I worked long enough and hard enough, then maybe I too could pull up a chair at life's feast. I had to believe that – or what would be the point?

After a couple of months of visits to the library with my mum, I started making trips by myself. Less than five minutes away from our house in Beckenham, it was the one place Mum and Dad would let me visit on my own. I attended Saturday morning pictures, but I always had to take my younger brothers with me. Reading was the only time I had all to myself. I'd make a packed lunch and head off towards adventure – literally. Most

Saturday afternoons were spent at the library, devouring books until closing time. Then I'd take out as many books as I could on my ticket and try to make the stories last until the next time I could visit the library again, usually the following weekend. The library began to feel like a home from home – a refuge that I could take ownership of because it was free for all to use. And it became increasingly needed, as the quarrels between Mum and Dad over his gambling grew more frequent. It was required when I fell out with one of my siblings or when the teasing about being ill all the time – being pathetically frail, not even able to stand up straight as I sometimes found it hard to lock my knees – grew too much to bear.

Whenever we moved home (which was often because, I learned years later, Dad had trouble passing a betting shop without stepping inside), the first place I sought out was the public library, and that's been the pattern ever since, well into adulthood. We lived in houses all over south-east London; New Cross, Beckenham, Brockley, Sydenham. I was lucky. At least one library in every new district was within a short walking distance from my house. Libraries made me a reader, a lover of stories and storytelling. A thinker. If it wasn't for public libraries, I truly believe I would never have become an author.

We had very few fiction books at home when I was growing up. Dad didn't believe in fiction. He was happy, or at least happier, to spend money on non-fiction books. They had a point and a purpose. Fiction books, not so much. We had a set of *Encyclopaedia Britannica*s, a book on nature and animals, a book on space, the planets and their moons, and a book on car mechanics. When I asked him once why he didn't rate fiction books, he replied, 'Because it's not real, it's not true. Lorie, you need to live in the real world.' He didn't understand that books helped me make sense of the real world and the fact that there were good and hateful people in it. Even at a young age, as I walked to school or to the library, some white adults told me to go back to where I came from. Once or twice, I even got elbowed off the pavement into the path of oncoming cars. Incidents such as these taught me to be aware of those around me, to cultivate the Black-girl equivalent of a spider-sense. Stories not only helped me to understand that there are good and bad people in the world, but taught me that not everyone who frowned at me was my enemy and not everyone who smiled at me was my friend.

Back at the library I read and read some more. In the mid-1960s, we moved to a maisonette in Brockley, then to a house in Sydenham in the early 1970s. Man landed on the moon – and I watched it, and then read about it. I searched out books about alien life forms on other planets and longed to meet some. Maybe they held answers that we on Earth were still striving to find. I loved books that took me to new places and spaces, that let me walk in the shoes of others who were different to me. I found no books that allowed me to walk in the shoes of those like me. But stories continued to be my passport away from parental quarrels and sibling arguments and doors slamming and feeling lonely.

By the time I started secondary school in 1973, I must have read several hundred books. I remember wondering why none of the books I read featured Black children in them. Not one of them featured a Black child like me. There were no children of colour whatsoever. In recent times I've heard some adults say that children don't notice these things. Well, that's nonsense. They do. This child did. Before me on the page was a world of literature that I loved, but it didn't reciprocate. It didn't even know I existed. The omission of 'me' on the page rendered my life, my existence unimportant. Irrelevant. I was invisible.

There was a literary feast going on 24/7 and if you were white, you could pull up a chair and have a seat at the table. I was outside the building looking in and watching others gorge themselves. When I read stories such as the *Chalet School* adventures by Elinor M. Brent-Dyer or C. S. Lewis's *Narnia* series, I would imagine myself as the protagonist. Even the fairy stories and myths and legends I read featured no characters of colour.

Each book was full of descriptions of characters with pale skin, milky skin, porcelain skin, alabaster skin, which blushed and flushed and turned red, and I would skim over those sentences. Such descriptions took me out of whatever story I was reading, not because the stories contained white protagonists but because *all* the stories I read featured white protagonists. I was nowhere. By extension I was nothing. My place in this world was not deemed worthy of recognition, recording, exploration or even comment. That's how it felt at the time.

As a child, the only Black people I saw in films and on TV were mammies and slaves in 1930s, 40s and 50s Hollywood films. Black women were presented as being of low intelligence and living as sex workers or solely for the care of their white charges. Men were presented as being of no intelligence and only good for being human donkeys, as comic relief or as criminals. These Hollywood films went round the world and countries with no indigenous Black population swallowed the nonsense they were being fed about Black people – there were no films to counter these depictions. This is not to disparage the Black actors of this era and earlier who had no choice in the roles they were offered, and hats off to Lincoln Perry for being the first Black actor in Hollywood to earn one million dollars. But his stage name and persona of the slack-jawed fool Stepin Fetchit used to make my face burn with mortification.

Now here we were in the 1960s and 70s and very little had

changed. Black people in TV and film were relegated to slaves, pimps and sex workers, with very few exceptions. Thank God for the late, great Sidney Poitier! In films like *Lilies of the Field*, *To Sir, with Love* and *In the Heat of the Night*, he played characters of intelligence and dignity. When I watched Sidney Poitier, I knew I'd experience no second-hand embarrassment. By the late 70s and early 80s, it felt like the decades had changed but the roles available to Black actors had not – at least not substantially. There were biopics, blaxploitation films or films about coping with being Black in a white world. *Plus ça change*.

In the contemporary literature of the time, we Black people were non-existent as main characters, at least in the UK. My imagination had to work overtime to place me within the stories I was reading. Without ever asking or being told, I thought I knew why there were no Black people in the books I was reading. It was because Black writers didn't exist! I genuinely believed that at the time. I had never seen any, heard of any, discussed any with friends and family or at school. I'd never seen Black people on the cover of any books, magazines or comics. Without being explicitly told as much, my place in society – as a third-class citizen – was being constantly reinforced.

I know this spurred my writing as an adult, and that one of the major reasons I became an author was the dearth of Black protagonists in books. If children's books featuring Black protagonists had been plentiful and positive when I was a child, what kind of writer would I be today? I wonder.

4

We writers are life vampires. We draw on real-life negative and positive experiences to write the truth into fiction. Do I use the experiences related to me by friends and acquaintances as the basis for my stories? No, I don't. Nor would I dream of doing so without permission. Do I use such retellings as inspiration to create my own stories? You better believe it. Isn't that a huge part of what the arts are? Doesn't art come from a blend of what we know of life, what we embrace, what we reject and what we hope for? A running from or a running to? Or maybe both. A number of stories contain moments when characters feel lost and alone and don't know which way to turn. I've written about characters who have felt exactly that at some point. When Callum in *Noughts and Crosses* feels severed from his hopes and dreams, he joins a terrorist organisation called the Liberation Militia. The things he is made to do as part of this group lead him to believe he is mentally and emotionally lost, cut adrift from the rest of society but with a specific goal in mind – equality for Noughts – to be accomplished by any means necessary. In *The Deadly Dare Mysteries*, I explore the idea of being both physically and mentally lost when Theo's best friend Ricky goes missing.

Writing about being figuratively or literally lost is not a total flight of the imagination for me. One sunny Saturday morning in the summer of 1968, when I was six years old, Dad announced we were going to visit some friends in Reading, whom none of us kids had ever met before. This was a couple of weeks after Martin Luther King Jr had been assassinated. At the time I had no real appreciation of who he was, only that Mum and Dad watched the news avidly every night (broadcast at the time in black and white) and discussed how Dr King had died and what the repercussions might be in America and in Britain. Around that same time, some guy called Enoch Powell gave a speech making it clear that he and his constituents didn't want us Black people in Britain. I didn't pay too much attention to what he or the newsreaders were saying. I was focused on plasticine model-making and playing tunes on the piano.

On that bright Saturday morning, the whole family set off in the car to drive to Reading. Wherever we went, the route was meticulously planned ahead of time and we never stopped off at restaurants or cafés along the way. It was years later that I realised why. In 1968, we weren't welcome. Dad would sometimes bring takeaways home from restaurants and again I didn't twig why for a long time. Restaurants didn't want to serve us. Black families were not welcome. Black people were not welcome. So we had homemade sandwiches or takeaways whenever we travelled. I didn't have a sit-down meal in a restaurant until my late teens.

Dad told us that the children we were going to meet were our cousins. It's a Bajan thing to address adults as Auntie-this or Uncle-that as a mark of respect. And their children were referred to as cousins. Being a blood relation had nothing to do with it. On arrival in Reading, we were greeted by a house full of warmth and laughter, food and people. It was a party, but I didn't know for whom or for what reason. I don't think I ever found out. The house was overrun with children, the atmosphere loud and fun. By mid-afternoon, my older brother and some of our cousins announced they were going for a walk, and

Dad insisted that they take me with them. Their expressions made it very clear that none of the boys wanted a little girl dragging around after them, but Dad was adamant – it was take me or not go. So off we went. We headed along the street to the main road, but the boys were walking fast. Too fast. Soon they were almost out of sight. I tried running after them, but they had disappeared. I looked around the street, a forest of legs surrounding me, and didn't have a clue how to find them. I decided to retrace my steps and head back to my cousins' house. Except I couldn't remember the route. I wandered up and down and turned a corner into a quieter road, but I didn't recognise it and thought better of heading in that direction. Turning this way and that, I watched as people flowed round me.

I was lost.

Not knowing what to do, I stood in the middle of the high street and burst into tears. Some people looked at me and moved on, some people looked straight ahead and walked round me. One man stopped and squatted down so that his face was level with mine. He was white, with beige-brown hair, dark brown eyes and a sympathetic smile.

'What's wrong?'

'I'm lost,' I cried. All lessons about not talking to strangers flew away from me.

'What's your name?'

'Lorie.'

'D'you remember your address?'

'I live in London. We are visiting cousins. They live in a house with a blue door.' I replied with the only detail of their house that I could remember.

'OK, that doesn't help much. Here,' he offered his hand. 'I'll help you find a policeman.'

Still crying, I took his hand as he led me along the street. I had no idea where we were going and could barely see through my tears. All I could see was the never-ending forest of legs. All I knew was that the stranger-man holding my hand was going to help me find my way home.

We'd only been walking for a couple of minutes when a voice bellowed out from behind us. 'Where are you going with my daughter? What d'you think you're doing?' Dad roared, puffing from running so hard.

'She was lost and crying,' the man explained rapidly. He let go of my hand like it was suddenly sun-core hot. 'I was just taking her to a police station.'

Dad eyed him, suspicion tightening his lips but relief lightening his tone. 'Thank you,' he said. 'I'll take her home now.'

Dad held out his hands and lifted me up. I don't remember much after that, except for my brother getting into a whole heap of trouble for abandoning me. But years later, as I look back on that incident, I wonder what happens to the alternative me, the one who wasn't found by my dad. In some parallel world, Malorie exists and is living her life – or not – in a world where she got lost and her dad didn't find her in time, and she walked off with the man who promised to take her to a police station.

And though the memory of getting lost isn't pleasant, I hold onto it as a research tool for my writing. Whenever I need to access the thoughts and feelings of someone who is lost, alone and scared, I just remember that time back in 1968 when I was six years old.

5

One of my favourite Stephen King films is *Misery*, starring Kathy Bates as Annie Wilkes. There's a scene where Annie is explaining her childhood obsession with going to the Saturday matinee (or Saturday pictures as it was called when I was growing up), where she watched the movie serial *Rocket Man*. She describes one particular episode, in which Rocket Man has been kidnapped and placed in a car heading towards a cliff. He doesn't make it out in time and the car goes straight off the edge and bursts into flames. Annie explains that each week's instalment began with a recap of what had gone before. And she remembers her indignation at the start of the following week's screening when, in the recap, the audience is shown Rocket Man escaping the car *before* it goes over the cliff. While every child is cheering, Annie gets up and proclaims, 'Have you all got amnesia? They just cheated us. He didn't get out of the cockadoodee car.'

Now, at the risk of sounding as bat-shit as Annie Wilkes, she does have a point. This was me growing up. I was not a fan of stories – in any form – that were illogical or inconsistent, that lacked continuity or took downright liberties like that.

If you were to ask me where my head was at in junior school, I'd answer in the clouds, or beyond the Earth surfing cosmic waves or exploring the myriad worlds of speculation and wonder. Basically, my head was all over the place. My imagination allowed me to roam across the universe and back, but along with that freedom came firm instructions from my mind about how I should do things. If I left home on a Monday leading with my left foot, my mind dictated that on Tuesday I step out of the house with my right foot – I didn't want either foot to get jealous or feel slighted, so I complied. That's where my head was. I told myself not to step on the cracks in the pavement, or, if I did step on cracks, every step until I got to school had to be on a crack. It was exhausting and time-consuming, but I did it.

As already mentioned, I felt a frustration with things that didn't make sense. I had no problem believing in the existence of aliens in the *Star Trek* TV series or the film *War of the Worlds*. Ghosts, demons, angels, monsters – I was quite prepared to believe in the possibility they might exist. Did Superman exist? Well, who was to say that a being from another planet in a different solar system wouldn't have superpowers if they found themselves on Earth? But watching the first *Superman* with Christopher Reeve, I remember getting vexed at the end of the film by the idea of Superman flying round and round the Earth faster and faster to reverse the orbit of Earth, and therefore to reverse time. Or the scene in the same film when Superman takes Lois Lane flying way up high in the Earth's atmosphere and she has no trouble whatsoever breathing.

Is it any wonder then that others found me intensely irritating?

There were certain behaviours and rituals I had to force myself to unlearn, to abandon, or at least to modify so that they would no longer rule my life. It was hard work forcing myself to ignore my clamouring mind when I walked on a crack in the pavement, or when I didn't. It was hard work learning to behave like everyone else for whom cracks in the pavement were not a trial to be overcome. I buried my true self until it became hidden, even from myself. It took time to reclaim that person, to realise her worth.

Because without her, I wouldn't have been able to write stories.

Without her, I'd see the world the same as other people who see as they're told to see, feel as they are instructed to feel, think as they're taught to think. Without the girl who was out of step with those around her, who writhed and thrashed against the mundane definitions of 'normal', what would there be to write about? It took me far too long to reclaim her, channel her eccentricities and let them flourish.

My mind is a kintsugi bowl. The cracks are the interesting bits, the parts filled with wonder, filled with stories and poems, filled with my own voice and my own way of looking at the world. It took years to appreciate that the cracks in my pavement are filled with gold.

That's who I was.

That's who I am.

Onwards and upwards.

6

When I was nine years old, my form teacher Mrs B announced that we would all be going into the hall to watch an opera. I looked at my best friend Ellie, unable to believe my ears – an opera? I wasn't the only one who thought this was a cruel and unusual punishment. Almost everyone in the class was horrified. What had we done to deserve it? As far as I was concerned operas were filled with dull, middle-aged white people and only appealed to a similar demographic.

Our protests were loud and long, until Mrs B had had enough and threatened the next person to moan at her with detention, which shut us all up. I walked into the assembly hall like I was walking to my execution. The entire class sat down on the floor cross-legged and waited for the boredom to begin. A tall, brunette white woman wearing a flowing black-and-red velvet robe came on stage and announced that we would be watching an operetta called *Hansel and Gretel*. Now, I had always loved fairy stories, myths and legends, epic tales like *Jason and the Argonauts* and *Sinbad* – but not in the form of an opera.

I wasn't expecting much as the music began to play. Less than five minutes into the production, aside from the music, you could have heard a pin drop. All eyes, and I mean *all* eyes, were glued to the stage. The actor who played the children's stepmother was the same woman who announced what we'd be watching – and she was amazing. She made her disdain for her children clear from the start, which meant all of us kids sympathised with Hansel and Gretel. She was so mean to them, inflicting random pinches and slaps, not feeding them the same food she ate. And as for the actor playing the witch who coaxed them into her house after the children were abandoned, she was absolutely terrifying. When she caged Hansel, making it clear that she was going to eat him as soon as he was fat enough, we all held our breath.

The combination of the music and the singing was sublime; we were all caught up in the drama. *Hansel and Gretel* was the perfect choice: the themes of abandonment and injustice and using your wits to get out of trouble were ones that every child could relate to. I was in awe of how the witch could be so evil. Sitting still for an hour and a half on cold, hard parquet flooring felt like sitting for five minutes on soft upholstered cushions. When the opera company finished, the applause that followed was thunderous. We had all seen something truly incredible and couldn't stop talking about it for days. In fact, we begged our teacher to bring the opera company back to do another show.

Before watching *Hansel and Gretel*, I had believed that opera was not for me. Even at nine years old, I had internalised the idea that opera was only for rich white people – because every time I saw it on the television, or even saw people talking about opera on the TV, everyone involved was white. The singers, the orchestra, the members of the audience – all white. That night I lay in my bed still buzzing from what I'd seen. I wondered about other forms of art that I'd previously considered were not for me, such as classical music, the Proms, Renaissance paintings and sculptures. Who were they made for, and why should I think I was excluded from them?

In March 2022, the *Guardian* published an article with the headline, 'Museum visits do not improve GCSE results, study reveals'. It cites a report in the *British Journal of Sociology of Education* concluding that cultural outings do not help secure higher grades, and challenging the notion that wealthy children have a leg-up in their education through routine exposure to the arts. The study suggests that there is no quantifiable data to prove that visits like these have any kind of beneficial effect.

'Bollocks!' I thought. As Albert Einstein is reported to have said, 'Not everything that counts can be counted, and not everything that can be counted counts.' Who is to say that a visit to an art gallery or a museum or an opera house or a play is not the key to unlocking some child's creativity? Who is to say that such a visit won't be the inspiration required for a child to think bigger and beyond, and to decide, 'I'm going to do that someday'? Watching *Hansel and Gretel* in primary school made me realise that I had just as much right to the arts, all the arts, as anyone else. I could take just as much enjoyment from them as anybody else. If Churchfields Primary School hadn't arranged for the opera company to come and perform for us, I might never have reached that realisation, or at least not until I was much older. But, as far as I can tell, theatrical groups and opera companies set up for school visits are now practically non-existent. Over the decades, I must have visited hundreds of schools nationwide. Too many teachers have informed me that arts subjects such as drama, music and dance tend to be the first to be cut when school resources are challenged.

How many children will have been deprived of making the discovery that art is for them and includes them because some schools simply don't have the wherewithal to fund these activities? It's so important to take the arts to children, and to allow them to access and enjoy the experience for free if their parents or guardians can't afford to pay the price of admission. Why should art only be the providence of those with depth to their pockets? I understand creative spaces are stretched beyond measure because of government cuts and dwindling resources, but we withdraw and ignore such spaces at our long-term peril.

In 1972, another memorable event happened at my primary school. A drama group visited us to put on a play about witches. We students weren't sure what to expect. Magic and mystery? Spells and suspense? We all sat in the hall in breathless anticipation. The actors emerged on stage wearing puritan costumes – long smocks, frilly socks, petticoats and ruff collars. They split us into three groups – farmers, labourers, and church elders – to work with the actors.

'What kind of magic is this?' I wondered with a frown.

The play started and there wasn't a wand or a single magic word to be seen or heard. The production was interactive and we were all a part of it. We were told we were living in a town in America in the seventeenth century, and that certain people in our community were under suspicion of practising witchcraft. Those accused were being put on trial and would be condemned to death if found guilty. But the accused were guilty until proven innocent, so their trials were strictly performative.

My class was invited to speak up and take part in the trial of the accused witches if we had something, anything, to say about what was going on. Within minutes we were all immersed in the drama unfolding. Three-quarters of the way through I was so angry I got to my feet and said, 'This is nonsense. This isn't fair. Where does this end? I could stand here and accuse everyone except me of being a witch. Are you then going to hang every single person here?' I sat down, livid. Others in my year also jumped up to protest along similar lines. We were so involved in the play that everyone started shouting over everyone else, declaring the proceedings to be bogus. Our outrage did no good. Those on trial were condemned to die by hanging, and one man was condemned to die by having heavy rocks placed on him until he could no longer breathe. Furious, I was just ready to jump up again when an actress stepped forward and asked us to take our seats off the stage. What was happening?

We all sat down. The hall fell silent. She proceeded to tell us the story of the Salem witch trials, the historical basis for the play we'd just taken part in: between 1692 and 1693, more than two hundred people had been accused of witchcraft in Salem, Massachusetts. Nineteen were executed by hanging – men and women, but mostly women – and one man was pressed to death.

The shock that reverberated around us was tangible.

'Oh my God,' I thought. 'We've been acting out real events.'

None of us could believe it. The actors lined up in front of us and took a bow. There was a brief moment of stunned silence, then the applause that rang out filled the hall to the high ceiling. There hadn't been applause like it since the *Hansel and Gretel* operetta. The actors got a spontaneous standing ovation.

Decades later, I still remember it as one of the most interesting, exciting, informative, eye-opening events I ever took part in at school. Did it improve my exam grades afterwards? No, not that I recall. Did it improve my life? Did it expand my thinking? Yes. Did it have a profound effect on me? Hell, yes. The impact of the arts on my life cannot be measured accurately in any report. How do you put a price, a monetary or quantifiable value, on something as real but nebulous as wonder? Taking part in the drama taught me something about speaking up when injustice is right under your nose. It taught me about how the persecution of a few can spread like an epidemic if it isn't checked.

I once visited a primary school in Brixton where the teacher told me in a loud voice in front of her class, 'Don't expect much from them because they're not very bright.' Two-thirds of her class were Black or brown. Another teacher said something similar when I visited a school in Dublin. The pupils in that Dublin class were all white. Both teachers were wrong – on so many levels. I did a creative writing workshop with the Year 6 class in Brixton, and they produced some of the most original, lyrical work I've encountered in any of the schools I've attended – both state and private. However, the entire time I was taking the workshop, the teacher sat in a corner of the class reading her newspaper. Appalling! She wasn't the slightest bit interested in her students or the work they were producing. Even now my heart bleeds for those children. They deserved so much better.

If my visit showed those children that authors can come in all shapes and sizes and from all backgrounds (something I didn't appreciate until my early twenties), then I'll have done my job. All I can hope is that some of the children in that creative writing workshop came away with the belief that maybe they too could write stories and poems.

At secondary school, I loathed hockey and netball but loved playing summer sports. I was in the tennis and rounders teams, and we often played against other teams in south-east London and beyond in interschool championships. Most of the time teams came to us, but sometimes we visited other schools to play our matches. One such rounders match was arranged with

Croydon High School, a private school and part of the Girls' Day School Trust. On the bright, sunny afternoon in question, we took a long minibus journey and, on arrival, were shown out onto the grounds where our rounders match would be held. This was the first time I'd ever visited a private school. My school, Honor Oak Grammar, had lovely grounds, a stream, our own science block and an excellent reputation but, oh my God, Croydon High School was next level. The grounds were huge, and the school had resources we could only dream of. And the girls who went there had a ready assurance, a self-belief that was fascinating to encounter. They didn't doubt for a second that they were going to win – and they were right. We lost our rounders match, in fact we got annihilated. And while they did have home-pitch advantage, the visit was a lesson in itself.

As an author, I've had the chance to visit numerous state and private schools, both primary and secondary, up and down the country. I have found no difference in intelligence or engagement regarding the children in most of the schools I've been to, but here's what I have found. Every private school I've visited – without exception – has had a dedicated library space with at least one full-time school librarian. Every private school I've visited has had a robust music, arts and drama programme. Most private schools have more resources than state schools, and I can't help but wonder about the possibilities and potential regarding all our children's futures if state schools were as well funded as private schools.

I grew up to realise that access to the arts is not just a cultural issue, it's a political issue. Successive governments have waxed lyrical about closing the social mobility gap, but talk is not just cheap – it's free. When it comes to children, access to the arts and resources to explore the sciences are obvious ways to narrow the gap between the haves and the have-nots. I find it sadly remarkable how we can always find the money to fund wars but never find the money to maintain peace or to improve the quality of children's lives.

7

Geek alert! In 1973, I really enjoyed taking my eleven-plus – the exam that decided whether or not I'd get into a grammar school. I loved the verbal reasoning tests in particular. Even the numerical tests were fun, and they didn't really feel like a test at all. If my family or teachers were nervous about my results, they never communicated that to me. I just got on with daily life until the day the results arrived – and I'd passed. I was told I could choose which grammar school to attend and was given a list of schools to select from, all within a few miles of our home in Brockley. The list read as follows:

Colfe's Grammar School
Prendergast Grammar School
Honor Oak Grammar School
Haberdashers Aske's Grammar School

As I loved forests and trees, and considered myself something of a tree hugger, I decided that Honor Oak sounded like it would suit me best. Honor Oak painted a picture in my head of greenery and centuries-old oak trees, of sprites beneath those trees and fields of daisies lying like summer snow on the ground. Plus, I liked the way the words sounded together. Honor Oak. The decision was as arbitrary as that. I chose my school because it had the most poetic name.

With the necessary forms sent off and my place confirmed, Dad took me to buy the uniform: a royal-blue shirt, a navy tie, skirt and jumper, and a navy blazer. There was even a matching navy beret, but I only ever wore that once as I found out no one else at the school bothered with it. Within a week, I knew I'd made the right decision. Honor Oak was a beautiful school, its red-brick buildings conferring a sense of tradition, but with up-to-date facilities and resources. It had its own science block, tennis and netball courts, and two large playing fields with a stream running between them. I had come from a primary school with tarmac for a playground, where the only green I remember came in the form of the coloured pencils and paints we sometimes used in art lessons. An added bonus was that only one other person from my primary school joined me, so it was my chance to forge a new identity. However, I was just a month into my new school when the wonder of attending a prestigious grammar school was tarnished for me.

Late one night when I couldn't sleep, I got out of bed and headed for the kitchen for a glass of water. I'd barely opened my bedroom door when I heard Dad's voice. He was in the living room, talking to my older brother and sister about me.

'You see that Malorie? She's turned into a right snob since she started going to that school,' said Dad.

I couldn't have been more hurt if he'd physically slapped me. I'd been so excited about attending Honor Oak that maybe, at first, I had gone on and on about it. But I soon learned only to talk about my forthcoming school if someone else brought up the subject first. I didn't talk about passing my eleven-plus or my new smart uniform – at least not as often as before. As far as I was concerned, life was to continue as normal, but the comments from some friends and some family made it clear that they expected me to change.

'Don't get too big for your boots,' they said.

'Don't go thinking you're better than the rest of us.'

Those and similar admonishments were lobbed my way, and I tried to volley them away with a smile or a shrug. But a few barbs hit me, and some hurt. What my dad said of me hurt most of all. He'd told me he was proud that I'd passed my eleven-plus and got into grammar school.

'With a good education behind you, there's nothing you can't do,' he said. 'But you'll still have to work twice as hard and be twice as good to get half as far.'

And now he was calling me out of my name behind my back. I went to bed and brooded on what I'd just heard. The next day at school, Dad's words were still playing on my mind. Throughout the entire day, I said very little. At home that same evening, before Dad got home from work, I said even less. I was so unusually quiet that Mum turned to me as I was eating my dinner and said, 'Child, what's wrong with you tonight?'

With tears rolling down my face, I said, 'Dad called me a snob because I go to a grammar school.'

Mum's eyes narrowed. 'Did he?'

I nodded.

An hour later, Dad had barely set foot in the house before Mum tackled him. 'How could you call your own daughter a snob?'

'What're you talking about?' asked Dad.

'The child says you called her a snob. That's not a nice thing to call your own daughter,' said Mum.

Dad marched into the living room where we were all seated, scattered around the room like wind-blown tree blossoms.

'How dare you tell lies?' Dad rounded on my elder sister and brother. 'I never said any such thing. If anything, I *want* your sister to turn into a snob.'

It was as if I were seeing him for the first time. There's a cinematographic technique used for dramatic emphasis called the dolly zoom, which creates a sense of unease or disquiet in the viewer. The shot is effective in focusing the viewer's complete attention. Well, that was me as I watched my dad insist that he hadn't called me a snob. I'd heard him call me that with my own ears and here he was ready to chastise my brother and sister for telling on him, or so he thought.

Nothing else existed in the room – in the world. Just him. My dad. Here was a grown man lying. I was stunned that he could look me in the eye and lie without blinking, and he was so convincing.

That was the moment my childhood innocence ended.

Loss

8

1975. I was thirteen years old. My older sister and brother no longer lived with us so it was just Mum, Dad, my younger brothers and me in our house in Sydenham. My older siblings had struck out on their own and now had their own places to live. It had been a strange June, with some parts of the UK experiencing snow. The school term was almost over, just a few more weeks to go, and I couldn't wait for the long summer break to start. I had my itinerary all worked out – long bicycle rides, lots of library visits, trips to the Horniman Museum and maybe even an outing or two to the West End. This would be my summer of exploration. I was thirteen and old enough to head off on my own and do my own thing. I was ready for adventure! There was a whole world out there just waiting for me to explore it, starting with south-east London.

On one of those last days of term, I woke up, had breakfast, went to school, attended lessons and walked home from school. It was a day much like any other. Nothing special, nothing different.

Until I got home.

I turned the key in the front door. And listened. Silence. Blessed, blissful silence. No shouting, no doors slamming, no loud TVs or louder radios.

'Hello?'

I was alone. *Yes!* I loved being the first home. Opening the door onto peace and quiet and no arguments about Dad's gambling was so relaxing. Being alone, I had my checklist to perform before I could truly settle. It was part of my after-noon routine when I was the first to arrive. A ritual to be carried out for peace of mind. But on this day, when I was eleven, I'd come home to find that we'd been burgled. We'd been cleaned out. The downstairs TV was gone, as was the TV in our kitchen that was shaped like an astronaut's helmet. Our gramophone record player, Mum's jewellery, even the kitchen radio was gone, as was our landline dial phone. I couldn't understand why anyone would want to steal our phone. The house was totally ransacked, with clothes and all our belongings strewn on the floor in every room. I ran from room to room feeling physically sick, then became terrified that the burglars were still in the house. They weren't. What should I do? I ran all the way to the high street and the nearest phone box to call for the police.

Since that time, I had made sure to perform my checklist if I was the first one home in the afternoon. I walked from room to room, mentally ticking them off in my head. Kitchen, living room, twins' bedroom, my bedroom, bathroom – check. All neat and tidy – and empty. I headed for Mum and Dad's bedroom. There was something unexpected in there.

An envelope taped to the dressing-table mirror with one handwritten word centred on the envelope in my dad's slanty handwriting: *Ruby*. My mum's name. I pulled the envelope off the mirror, took out the single sheet of folded paper inside and began to read. With each word, my blood ran cold.

Dad was leaving Mum.

He was leaving all of us. He wanted out, so he'd walked. Just like that, leaving us behind. In a daze of quiet but intense panic, I replaced the sheet of paper – half filled on one side with handwriting that outlined accusations, recriminations and justifications – in its envelope. I put the envelope back on the mirror, making sure the glass was slightly tilted, just as

I'd found it. I matched up the sticky tape to the mark it had made on the mirror, just as I'd found it. I had an impulse to tear it off and rip it up and put it in the bin. Mum would never know. Then she wouldn't get upset and I could pretend, we all could pretend, that Dad would be home at any minute. Any moment.

I reached for the letter, but before making contact my hand dropped to my side. I knew I couldn't do that, no matter how much I might want to. Mum had to know the truth. I had no right to change that. Even at thirteen I knew that much. I wanted to stand in front of the juggernaut that was the truth and push it back to stop it from running over Mum and crushing her. From crushing us all.

But I couldn't.

So I left the letter on the mirror and went to my room. I lay on the bed, staring up at the ceiling, too heartsick to even shed a tear. All I could do was wonder what was going to happen to us as I waited for Mum to come home.

When at last Mum did get in from work, she went to her room and then . . . silence. My brothers were home from school by this time and the house was no longer quiet, but Mum's room was soundless. She was in her bedroom for a long, long time. When she finally emerged, she made our dinner of spaghetti bolognese without saying a word. My brothers didn't notice. I did. I waited all evening for Mum to say something. But she didn't. Not one word. A child can live, grow old and die in the spaces between the words that parents don't say.

The next day I went to school, wondering when or even if I'd ever see my dad again.

When I got home, Mum was already in the house ahead of me, which was unusual. I was normally the one who got home first.

But Mum wasn't alone. Bailiffs had descended like court-appointed vultures and they wanted us out. We had to leave. ASAP. They wanted us gone. They explained that the mortgage hadn't been paid and the house was being repossessed. Apparently the bank had sent letters. Mum hadn't seen them and I knew there'd been nothing about the house being repossessed in the letter Dad had written to Mum and stuck on the mirror. As far as the bailiffs were concerned, that didn't matter. We had to leave.

Get out.

Go.

At once.

Just like that, a hole opened and the bottom dropped out of my world.

And I plummeted.

9

Security is such a tenuous thing, isn't it? That feeling of waking up with nothing to worry about, nothing pecking away at your thoughts. I realised that security wasn't just about physical safety, it was also a state of mind.

It had taken me a long time to feel secure in our home after the burglary a couple of years earlier, but I'd finally reached that point. I no longer had dreams about waking up in the middle of the night to find an unfamiliar man peering over me. On days when I was the first one home, I no longer braced myself as I opened the front door in case I was confronted by a stranger. Home was once again my sanctuary. School, homework, reading and riding my bike once again occupied my mind.

The day before the note on the mirror was the last day I woke up feeling all was OK with the world. Not perfect, not great, but at least OK. After that, not so much, not for a long, long time. Trying to feel safe, secure and settled felt like trying to pin down a cloud with my little finger.

The bailiffs arrived and they weren't going to leave before we did, no matter how much Mum pleaded.

'Where are we meant to live?' Mum asked. 'What about my children? Where are we supposed to go?'

'I'm sorry, but that's not our problem,' one of the bailiffs replied. 'We have our job to do. You have to leave.'

Mum told me and my brothers to go and pack a small bag of essentials.

'What about my comics, Mum?'

Mum gave me a hard look. 'I said *essentials*.'

And that was that.

Being evicted from your home without warning does a number on your head, on your life and on your history. We were given one hour to get out. One hour to pack up a lifetime. I had the task of sorting out what to take with me and what to leave behind. Nothing heavy or bulky could be taken with us.

I kept asking, 'Where are we going to go, Mum? What're we going to do?'

Mum didn't answer. She couldn't. She didn't know.

In one sacred corner of my bedroom, I had an open box that was one metre high and about half a metre wide. It was filled to the brim with DC Comics, EC Comics and British comics; *Judy, Jinty, Bunty, Mandy*, plus *Spiderwoman, Catwoman, Batwoman, Rose and Thorn, Lois Lane, Superman, Spiderman, Tales from the Crypt, Suspense Comics, Tales of the Supernatural, The Vault of Horror, Crime SuspenStories, Shock SuspenStories* and a host of others. They were all my comfort reads, the stories I returned to again and again whenever I felt in need of a shield against the real world. Shield, hell! Whenever I felt the need of a force field against the real world. A force field against Mum and Dad's constant arguments about money at home, the bigoted comments from some at my school – including a couple of teachers – and the relentless news about the National Front party and their supporters marching up and down the country to tell me and others like me that they hated our guts and that we didn't and would never belong.

My comics were my most prized possessions, but I couldn't carry them all. I tried to search through them for my favourites, for the ones that I read the most, the ones that patched up the holes reality shot through my armour, but Mum entered my bedroom to check on my progress and, when she saw what

I was doing, told me I couldn't have them. Not one of them. There wasn't time to select favourites. Pack some clothes and some shoes. Essentials. Priorities. Stories were friends but they weren't essentials. Leave the comics alone. More than my tiny TV, more than my few toys, more than almost anything in my room, my comics were the belongings I hated leaving behind the most. Everything else was replaceable. My comics were not. The ones I'd had for years would never be available again. One last look at them, one last touch as if to absorb each and every story and I turned away, determined not to look at them again. I pulled clothes out of my wardrobe and out of my chest of drawers, selecting enough to fit into two carrier bags. Less than an hour later, we were out of the house with the bailiffs changing the front door locks behind us. They couldn't even wait for us to make it to the gate before they got to work. The front lock was being unscrewed and replaced while we were on the garden path. I took a final look at the home that was no longer ours. I drank in its white pebble-dashed brickwork and its black gloss-painted door, instinctively knowing that I would never see it again. Then my brothers and I followed Mum as we walked to the main road.

We were homeless.

10

The days that followed passed in a nightmare blur. We spent a day or two at my aunt's house in Tooting, south-west London, which was far too small to take us all. Mum camped on the doorstep of the local council pleading with them to give us somewhere to live.

Less than a week later we gathered up our belongings from my aunt's house and were on the move again. After travelling on at least three buses we arrived at our new home. We stood outside the block of flats for the homeless – and I was appalled.

The homeless shelter was a four-storey U-shaped building consisting of a number of flats per floor. Each front door and the steel guard rails that skirted the upper levels were painted the same deep, dark, cold blue. It had a small concrete court-yard. It made me think of a prison block. There was no lift so we climbed the stairs to the third floor, where Mum opened the front door to our new 'home'.

The first thing to hit me was the raucous band of noxious smells. There was a pungent smell of urine on bass, damp on keyboards and stale sweat on drums. The door opened straight onto the living room, which had a threadbare blue carpet, a filthy grey fabric sofa and, in one corner, a two-ring electric hotplate. We didn't even have an oven, just the hotplate – our only way to prepare a hot meal. There wasn't a fridge either. We walked through the flat in less than a minute in stunned, devastated silence. There was the living room, two bedrooms with bare beds and a small wardrobe in the slightly larger room, and a bathroom. The bathroom contained a once-white bath-tub now permanently stained brown, a filthy toilet and a sink to match. Black splotches decorated the upper corners of the room and the paint beneath the windowsill. We walked back out into the living room.

My brother John said what I was thinking. 'I hate it here.'

'I want to go home,' said James.

'This is our home now,' Mum replied, her expression grim.

We had no choice but to stay. We wiped down the mattresses and spent our first night in the homeless shelter sleeping in our day clothes. My brothers shared one bedroom, Mum and I had the other. That first night, I hardly slept. It hit me that we'd been dumped like last week's rubbish in a third-floor, two-bedroom flat in a homeless shelter. It was a place for the noth-ings of nowhere; the deserted and the destitute, the forlorn and the forgotten, the broken and the bereft. That's what I felt as I lay awake with cold, hard reality continuously punching at my head.

This homeless shelter was within five minutes of Lewisham Registry Office, Library and Hospital. Lewisham Shopping Centre was a fifteen-minute walk away. Outside, the world con-tinued to spin as normal. Inside, my whole world had stopped.

In the days that followed, Mum scrubbed the flat from top to bottom – the windows, the furniture, the bathroom with its cracked pane of glass and circular vent fan badly fitted into the window – but no amount of scouring could change a sow's ear into a Louis Vuitton purse. I learned on my first full day in the flat that it was infested with cockroaches. Every time a piece of furniture was moved, out they would scurry. I was cleaning my teeth and saw one run along the bottom of the bathtub beside me, heading for the plughole.

On our second day, I found out we had mice when one

scuttled across the living-room carpet. I took to sleeping with the blanket pulled up over my head so nothing could run into my ears or over my face.

We were stony broke and one step away from sleeping on park benches or in shop doorways. And every day I lived in fear that we'd be thrown out of our meagre flat and that's where we'd end up.

The only reason we survived at all was because of my mum.

We lived on cornflakes for breakfast, when we had milk, and streaky bacon and fries for dinner. My mum called them fries but more like dumplings than skinny chips – a mix of self-raising flour, sugar and water rolled into a ball, then flattened and fried in oil until cooked through and brown on the outside. Bacon and fries, fries and bacon – every day for months. There was no money for anything else. Though the homeless shelter was four storeys high including the ground floor, to me it felt like a hole. The emergency homeless centre was a landfill of desperate people.

Mum couldn't afford the laundrette so she washed our clothes in the bathtub. Drying them during the summer months wasn't too much of a problem because the flat was like an oven as the windows didn't open. In winter, air drying our clothes didn't work. There was no central heating, so Mum had been given an Aladdin paraffin heater. One. For the four of us. The heater was a metal box container with a reservoir into which the liquid paraffin was poured. When the wick was lit with a match it generated modest heat that was channelled out of the front grille of the heater. Every other day in winter, Mum carried home a heavy container of liquid paraffin. The heater provided some warmth within a metre radius but the stink of burning paraffin was awful – a chemical, nauseating odour which, to this day, flips my stomach and makes me feel sick. My sense of smell is particularly strong so entering the flat was bad enough at the best of times, but entering it when the heater was burning felt like torture.

In winter, especially, my school clothes reeked of damp and paraffin, so I tried to stay away from my school friends as much as possible. During breaks I would hide in the piano room in the music wing or at the back of the library, just so others wouldn't have to smell my home situation on my uniform. The standard of my schoolwork plummeted but I clung on to attending school for the respite it offered from the homeless shelter.

And I never told anyone. Not my friends, none of the teachers, no one.

No one said a word about my disappearing acts or the occasional sullen silences when the 'everything-is-fine-in-my-world' act would slip. If anyone did think that I smelled peculiar, they never said so to my face. At the time, I believed my homelessness was something to be ashamed of. And though it was not her fault, I also blamed my mum for not having a bank account and resources of her own, even though this was something that Dad had actively discouraged.

I walked to and from my secondary school, almost three miles each way, every day. As I had no money for bus fares, I had no choice. There were days when I walked home silently crying with tiredness. And there were many nights when I just cried. At school, I donned a mask that was a full-on permanent smile the moment I walked through the gates. I might've been crying inside but no way did I want my friends and teachers knowing that all wasn't well. I would've found that mortifying. Humiliating. The mask must've been a good one because none of them ever suspected.

Being evicted wasn't just about losing our home. It went deeper than that. We lost our security, our sense of space and

place. We had nothing to call our own. I couldn't even remin-
isce about happier times by looking at the photos of our past
life – we'd had to leave them behind when the bailiffs evicted
us from our house in Sydenham. All Mum had was one photo
of me as a four-year-old, a couple of pictures of my siblings –
and that was it. That's the only remaining photographic record
of our childhoods.

'This isn't permanent,' Mum kept saying. 'I'm not going to
let them dump us here and then forget about us.'

I couldn't only pray that she was right about our accom-
modation being temporary. In the meantime we lived off welfare benefits, which kept us from starving, but only just. Mum
spent her days going into shops, visiting factories and scan-
ning the newspapers looking for a job. When she wasn't doing
that, she was at the council offices trying to get us somewhere
better to live. Well, it's the squeaky wheel that gets greased,
because one day Mum came home and told us that we would
be moving out of the homeless shelter. We were all overjoyed.
I had visions of us getting a decent home similar to the one we
had in Sydenham.

In the spring of 1976, we were finally moved to a ground-floor
flat in Forest Hill, south London. The flat had a long corridor
running the length of the property, with each room situated
off the right of the corridor only. Again, I was put in mind of a
prison – with cells off the main walkway. The kitchen was at the
far end of the corridor next to the bathroom. The living room,
closest to the front door, served as my bedroom at night. And
once again, our only visitors were cockroaches, silverfish and
mice. Another dump.

Spring was burned away by summer, which in 1976 was
a scorcher. Baking-hot days followed by sweltering nights
in a flat where the windows didn't open and there was no

ventilation – except in the bathroom via a pull-string extractor fan in the window.

We weren't in the homeless shelter any more but this place wasn't much better. The pest infestation was even worse. Every day after school, I entered the flat with a lead-heavy heart. The only difference between here and the homeless shelter was that I didn't have to look up and down the street to make sure that no one I knew was in sight before entering the building. It resembled any of the other houses in the street, albeit a long and narrow version of them. But it certainly wasn't a place I would dream of bringing any of my friends back to. The last time I'd had friends over to my house was when we lived in Sydenham, which seemed like several lifetimes ago.

I hated the long-corridor flat.

I hated my life.

Was this it? Was this all there was or would ever be to my life?

I couldn't concentrate. I couldn't think straight. I was always cold and hungry, or hot and hungry, and was constantly worried that I and my school clothes still smelled terrible. I spent a lot of lunchtimes in a music practice room tinkering on a piano, or at the back of the school library, doing homework or reading. The school library and my nearest public library were more than just repositories of books; they were lifelines. Godsends. A warm, safe home away from a defective home. I truly believe that if it wasn't for them, I wouldn't be here now. I spent as many evenings as possible in my local public library, grateful for its warmth, its comfort, its promise of better things to come. I read Mills and Boon romances for their happy endings, devoured Agatha Christie crime novels because the criminals never got away with it, and sought out books like *Lace* by Shirley Conran and *Scruples* by Judith Krantz. These became my go-to escapist reads; they spoke of heroines who had nothing, and who used their brains and sheer determination to work their way through adversity and find a measure of happiness. It was a message I needed to hear. I read book after book that promised adventures and better times ahead if I just hung in there.

In the flat, when I wasn't reading, I listened to the radio, losing myself in music. We had no TV so relied on the radio for music and the news. It was the year of Stevie Wonder's *Songs in the Key of Life* and hits like 'Silly Love Songs' by Wings and 'Moonlight Feels Right' by Starbuck. Whenever I heard the marimba solo in the latter song, I'd stop what I was doing and listen as it invariably cheered me up. Falling in love with the songs I heard on the radio in 1976 became one of the few highlights I can recall from that difficult year.

Autumn gave way to winter and once again Mum had to trek out for liquid paraffin on a regular basis. The flat was so long that we'd been provided with an extra paraffin heater, but I'd lie in bed at night with my light on and could see my breath forming a cloud above me.

We stayed for months in Forest Hill with Mum still trying to find a job. It truly felt we'd been abandoned – by everyone – and left to rot. I studied hard, determined to get good grades in my O-level exams with a view to getting a decent job afterwards. It seemed like the only way out of our predicament, the only light at the end of a dark tunnel. There were many days when that light was barely a dot on the horizon. But when hope is all you have, you cling to it like a drowning person who is thrown a lifebelt.

The homeless years clarified one thing, though. I swore on everything holy that when I was older, I would never, *ever* rely solely on one person for my money and my living. I made a vow that if I ever got out of poverty prison, I wouldn't rely on anyone else for my happiness. I would be an independent woman who earned and owned. From that moment on, my happiness was going to lie entirely within my own hands. As far as I was concerned, happiness was just another word for money. And I'd find my way out of the landfill of us people who society was content to leave behind – by whatever means necessary.

II

From the age of fourteen, I worked weekends and throughout the school holidays to help with the household bills. One of those early jobs was as a Saturday girl at British Home Stores (BHS) in Peckham when I was sixteen. By this time, we'd been moved out of our flat in Forest Hill to a house in Lewisham. The house had three bedrooms, a living room, kitchen and a box room at the back which we used for storage. The walk to school was even longer from Lewisham, but I didn't mind because it felt good to be back in a house again, even though it had no central heating and needed a lot of renovation work. At least in this house we didn't have to contend with cockroaches, for which I was grateful.

At BHS in Peckham, I worked as a cashier as well as in other departments within the clothes section. Every Saturday morning, bright and early – or early at any rate – I'd hop on a 36 bus from Lewisham and within the hour I'd be at work. In those days all the Saturday staff had to take a maths test to make sure we could handle the tills and would give customers their correct change. I enjoyed working on the till, but what I enjoyed even more was the independence that having a job gave me. I felt useful, like I was helping Mum by paying for my own schoolbooks and clothes as well as helping out with some of the bills. Plus, working in public-facing jobs gave me a real insight into human nature – the unexpectedly good, the covertly bad and the downright ugly. It was a life lesson in the way some people treat those who work in positions deemed 'less important' – minimum-wage positions in the service industries, for example. In a number of my holiday jobs, I was treated as if I had no value or ambition beyond what I was doing.

During the school summer holidays of 1978, as well as my Saturday job, I started working throughout the week as a catering assistant at a BT telephone exchange on Lisle Street in the West End. I'd arrive at seven-thirty each morning to cook and serve breakfast, tidy up, and then help to serve lunch, finishing each day at four o'clock in the afternoon. The catering staff were all women, except for the kitchen porter, and most of us were also Black. The majority of the engineers at the BT exchange were white men. Most of them were polite and civil. Some, however, were not and had no problem making their disdain for the serving staff obvious. Not knowing anything about us, they looked down on us because of the colour of our skin and our apparent lack of qualifications.

There was one man who lived to make my life a misery, so much so I referred to him in my head as Mr Misery. He was lean, with mid-brown hair, moss-green eyes and mean, almost non-existent lips. I used to dread his presence in the food hall.

One morning, he reached the front of the queue and I asked him politely, just as I did everyone else, what he would like to eat.

'Two fried eggs, toast, bacon and two sausages,' he replied. No sign of a 'please'.

The bacon and sausages were in large serving trays before me, ready to be placed on plates as required. The eggs I was expected to fry when asked for. So I cracked two eggs on the oiled griddle while Mr Misery stared a hole into me as I worked. I placed the toast on the plate, then the bacon, sausages and finally the eggs and handed it to him. He refused to take it.

'I'm not taking that. I can't eat that,' he proclaimed.

My heart sank. 'Here we go again,' I thought.

'What's wrong with it?' I asked.

'Look at those eggs. They're disgusting and the yolks are too pale.'

'I fry them, I don't lay them. D'you want them or not?'

Behind him, his colleagues started laughing. Mr Misery glanced at them before turning back to me, his eyes sparking with anger. He snatched up his plate and moved on. I knew he'd pay me back for my sarcasm. It was just a matter of when.

Lunchtime came and I clocked Mr Misery approaching the front of the queue with purpose. He chose his main course, which was served by my colleague, and moved to the station where I was serving the puddings.

'What's that?' he pointed at the tray of puddings in front of him. Each tray came with a sign stating what was on offer, so he already knew the answer. It was clear he was after blood.

'Apple crumble,' I replied. 'Would you like some?'

'Go on then,' he ordered.

I took the serving spoon and started to place a portion in a dessert bowl.

'I don't know how you've got the nerve to serve something like that,' he said. 'It's as dry as a stick.'

'Would you like some custard?' I asked.

'Yes,' he snapped.

'Well, when I put the custard on, it'll be wet, won't it?'

Mr Misery glared at me while everyone behind him in the queue fell about laughing.

He straightened up. 'With a remark like that, I'm not surprised you're working behind that counter.'

My jaw dropped. Mr Misery snatched up his bowl and smirked at me before walking off. It was on now! I wasn't going to take such snobbery and certainly not from this arsehole, but he was sitting down at his table by the time I had thought of a suitable retort. I suffer badly from *esprit de l'escalier* – that dilemma where you think of the perfect response but way too late. That's always been one of my problems. I can come up with excellent repartee but minutes, hours or sometimes days after the event. But I wasn't going to let this guy get away with insulting me without at least trying to speak up for myself – especially when it was not so long ago that I'd felt I had no voice at all.

The following day, I waited impatiently for Mr Misery to appear in front of me. When at last he did, I asked as I handed over his plate of sausages, fried egg, bacon and toast, 'Excuse me, but how many O levels do you have?'

'Four,' he replied.

'I have nine,' I said.

'Nine? Yeah, right,' he scoffed.

'Yes, nine. Would you like me to list them?' And it would've been ten if I'd managed to get higher than a D for my geography O level but he didn't need to know that.

'If you've got nine O levels, what're you doing working behind that counter?' asked Mr Misery, still sceptical.

'This is a summer job. I'm back at school in September to do my A levels. Then I'm off to university,' I told him. Well, OK, so that last bit wasn't necessarily true but he didn't need to know that either. He glared at me. I scowled right back.

'Maybe one day, you might even be working for me, tosser!' I thought with malicious glee.

Mr Misery looked me up and down, took his plate and left without a word. I carried on serving breakfast, but from that day on I carried myself with a renewed sense of purpose. I resolved to try hard not to judge people according to their so-called status, or their clothes, or the way they spoke or looked. Mr Misery assumed I was lower than him because of my job and, worse still, that I wasn't worthy of respect, kindness or consideration because of it. It's a life lesson that has stayed with me.

Somewhere in the multiverse, there's a me who swore at Mr Misery and lost my job. And there's another me who didn't pass her O levels and had to put up with arseholes defining me by the lack of exams officially passed. Working in service industries opened my eyes to facets of human nature – for which I'm grateful, as it equipped me with the tools to create believable characters in stories.

When dealing with other people, every day is a school day.

12

There's something about the memory of being stony broke that never leaves you, even if you subsequently manage to make a living. I have certain behaviours, some of them no doubt irritating to my family, which absolutely come from not having much as a teen – and living by the mantra of 'use it up and wear it out' regarding the little I did have.

I use a particular brand of body lotion which is fairly thick without being oily or leaving any residue (sorry to sound like an advertisement!), plus I like its scent. The plastic bottle it comes in is about twenty centimetres high. Being somewhat viscous, the lotion sticks to the sides of its container. A trick I learned when I was skint was to cut the bottom off the bottle, about six centimetres from the end, then use my finger to wipe around the inside. The part I've cut off then becomes the new lid for the bottle as it just squeezes over the now open end to ensure that it doesn't dry out. Once I've used up all I can from the new lid, and as far down as my finger can reach in the container, I cut off the now-used-up middle third and discard that, to enable access to the last third. That way the bottle of lotion lasts at least another four or five days. Another trait I've acquired is that I hate to see an empty fridge in my own home, so I try to make sure there's always more than just a litre of milk there. I'm blessed that I now have the wherewithal to keep my fridge stocked. It makes me appreciate having a choice of what to eat for dinner instead of just the fries and bacon, bacon and fries that Mum used to make.

The thing about losing everything is that you never shrug off the knowledge of how easy it is to find yourself in that predicament. Being homeless made me determined not to skip a single month of paying my rent or mortgage, even if it meant I didn't eat. Having little taught me a number of tips and tricks for making what I have last. TV programmes about bailiffs evicting people from their homes hit that much harder. Reports on homelessness or the rising use of food banks are felt more intensely. And when writing about characters who have lost everything, a lot less imagination is required.

There's a huge difference between living simply and living in poverty. There is nothing noble or ennobling about poverty. It sucks. It's like a steel trap that you'd gnaw off your own leg to escape. The falsehood that if you work hard enough you can escape poverty is insulting – especially if you work multiple jobs and still struggle to survive. Sometimes sheer will and hard work just aren't enough when luck isn't on your side.

There are some who look at successful people and assume that luck alone allowed them to prosper. But so much sheer hard graft goes into 'being lucky', and sometimes creating your own luck involves taking huge risks, like giving up paid employment to become self-employed in pursuit of a dream that is tenuous at best, or putting aside the wants and dreams of family to be true to yourself.

I'm a planner. When I gave up my computing job in my twenties, I created a one-year and a five-year strategy to assess what to do if my proposed future career as an author didn't pan out. I considered whether I would return to the world of computing or perhaps try to enter the world of books in some capacity, maybe as a bookseller or a librarian. But I didn't want to create a detailed plan B because then I might use it as an excuse to not pursue my plan A – being an author – to the fullest.

However, even taking a risk requires the wherewithal to do so. It requires a support mechanism, a safety blanket, and not everyone has that. Money isn't necessary to fulfil your dreams, to eat well and be mentally and physically healthy, but by God it helps. Income isn't a force field against unhappiness, but the comfort zone it provides can't be dismissed.

Whenever someone living in a bubble of wealth opens their mouth to offer a critique for how people below the poverty line should live their lives, I roll my eyes so hard I can see my optic nerves. The take is too often, 'You're not doing poorness right. Let me tell you how it should be done.' Not *show* you how it should be done. Never *show* you. Just tell you.

I believe in walking a mile in someone else's shoes before offering up an opinion or judgement on their lives. As Oscar Wilde said, 'To recommend thrift to the poor is both grotesque and insulting. It's like advising a man who is starving to eat less.'

Being poor is bloody hard work.

Robbing Peter and Paul to pay utility bills. Walking everywhere because you can't afford bus or train fare. Waiting till the shops are closing to pick up food at cheaper prices. Checking the price of every tin, every packet before it goes in your shopping basket. Maxing out credit cards and always being overdrawn. Staring up at the ceiling at night, wondering how you'll get through the next day or week, never mind the following month or year.

The list goes on. And on.

The worry is relentless. It doesn't stop.

Poverty and hunger are political. Choosing whether to provide food for poor children during the school holidays is a political decision. Building more – or any – social housing is a political decision.

If I was in charge, no MP would be able to hold a position in a state department without first having experience of their remit in the real world: full-time and for at least three months. You want to be secretary of state for education? Spend three months teaching or at least observing a classroom, *every single day*. Want to be secretary of state for transport? Travel to and from work by bus or train every day for three months, minimum. Travel up, down and across the country at different times of the day and night. Want to oversee the NHS? Work on the front line for three months. Go out with ambulance crews, work and observe what goes on in an A&E department. Be responsible for allocating ward beds to A&E patients. Go out and about with carers and see first-hand the care they are expected to provide in the short amount of time allocated to each person in their charge. You want to be the culture secretary? Grasp that it is the myriad forms and voices in the arts that enrich them and then ensure they are available for all to enjoy. And if you want to be chancellor of the exchequer? I'd give you a minimum-wage salary to live off for three months in winter, in a flat for which you have to pay rent and bills, plus buy food, plus travel expenses, plus maybe childcare – at the very least.

There is no substitute for insight born of experience. Too many of our politicians don't have a clue. It took me a very long time to realise that too many of them don't want one either.

Just sayin'.

13

When I was fourteen,
A school ski trip
Was announced.
The cost was three digits
But in the low three digits.
Might as well be
Ten digits
When you're broke.

A meal for a tenner,
Might as well be
A meal
For 10,000 pounds,
When you haven't got
A single spare pound
To call your own.

I took the letter home
Hope in my heart
Like a guttering flame.
Hope in my thoughts
That I could go
With all my friends
On the skiing trip.

I stood in our house
For the homeless,
And looked in the fridge
That only contained
A packet of bacon
and a pint of milk.
I shied away from
Inspecting the mould
On the walls and around
The windows.

I stood in our house
For the homeless,
And hoped.

I handed the letter
To Mum.
'Can I go?' I asked.
'Please can I go?'
Mum looked at me.
She didn't say a word,
Just looked at me.
I had my answer.

She handed back the letter.
I put it in the bin.
It was never mentioned again.

All my friends went on the ski trip.
I was one of only two students in the class
Who didn't go.
We were allowed to do extra reading

In the library,
All day long.

I read books that took me to
Faraway places
And spaces.
The troubled past,
The hopeful future.
I read books where I could be rich
And go anywhere
Do anything
Be anyone I wanted.

Books and my imagination
Took me all over the world,
Around the galaxy
Across the universe.
I could turn into anything
Be anyone
Do anything
As I sat in the library,
Reading,
While my friends
Went skiing.

When you have money
You can pick and choose.
To free-range or
Not to free-range
Is not even a question.
To organic
Or not to organic,

To adopt outdoor-reared
Or not to adopt the outdoors,
All turn on a whim
And a shrug of the shoulders.
Or sit as a belief,
A resolve,
That requires money
To even contemplate.

When you have money
You can pick and choose
Last year's fashion
Or this year's trends.
You can bang on
About being bang on.
This holiday spot
Or that villa let.
All-wheel drive,
Or plug-in hybrid,
Is the only headache,
Solved with a credit limit
And blue-bottled water.

When you don't have money,
Your food comes
With yellow stickers.
If it comes at all.
You shop at the end
Of the day,
When the bargains
Creep out to play

In the reduced-price
Food bins.

When you're broke
It's not a choice
Of eating or heating.
You can't do either.
So you drink a lot of water
To fill yourself up.
You crunch on cream crackers
That take a long time
To chew
    and swallow.
It fools your stomach into believing
It's receiving
More weight,
More mass,
More substance,
Than is really there.

When you're broke.
Life is an arithmetic game
Of survival.
When you're broke.

14

1976.

Daydreaming became my superpower. If 'what if?' were an Olympic sport, I could've won a gold medal.

What if I . . .?

I asked myself that question continually. What if I were invisible? What if I could fly? What if I could read minds? What if I knew instinctively when someone was lying? What if I could move objects with the wave of a finger, directed by the power of my thoughts? What if I lived in a home with radiators and a full fridge and didn't have to worry about anything but lessons and exams?

What if?

Being a daydream believer meant I was happy with my own company. Being alone didn't bother me. Well . . . not always. Being lonely did. Sometimes. But everyone got lonely sometimes.

Didn't they?

The what-ifs came thick and fast when we were homeless. I retreated into my imagination and tried to stay there for as long as possible. But real life kept dragging me out of my comforting reveries.

With my various part-time jobs, sometimes, just sometimes, I saved enough to treat myself to a new book or a trip to the cinema. Having some money to spend on such treats – even sporadically – allowed me to start looking outwards, rather than constantly focusing inwards, morosely shuffling my feet at my pity party for one.

I loved the cinema, the shared experience of watching films. Saturday morning pictures, attended from the time I was five or six, had ignited that passion. Each Saturday viewing was a visual blast, starting with *Looney Tunes Cartoons* and followed by an episode of *Flash Gordon*, which always ended on a cliffhanger. Then came the main feature film. It was on these golden Saturday mornings that I first encountered *Dr Who and the Daleks*, starring Peter Cushing, and *Jason and the Argonauts*. I'm reinforcing my age here, but when I was five or six, Saturday morning pictures cost a sixpence.

The very first film I watched outside of Saturday morning pictures was *Oliver!* (based on Dickens's *Oliver Twist*) at a cinema in Penge. My sister Wendy took me to see an evening showing and there was a different atmosphere as adults were present. It was less rowdy and more subdued. *Oliver!*, however, was a revelation. I *loved* it, though when Nancy died I cried my eyes out. It was my first memory of watching a film where one of the main characters unexpectedly died. After that I went to the pictures with my sister as often as I could, not just on Saturday mornings. Being in a cinema with a group of people sharing the same experience, having our emotions flipped at the same moments, was magical to me. Like newly discovering a song or a book that you're desperate to share and talk about. And even if you don't get to talk about it, just knowing that others have had the same experience is special. But there were so many films I wanted to watch that no one else in my family was interested in, so I started to go by myself. Alone. And it was fine – until the day that it wasn't.

When I was fourteen, I decided to blow all my spare money on a film. I paid for my ticket and took my seat in the huge auditorium, waiting for Disney's *Robin Hood* to start. Robin Hood and Little John were just walking through the forest – what a day – when three white boys in their mid to late teens sat directly behind me. They were whispering and laughing among themselves. I glanced behind and immediately my antennae began to quiver. Any woman who enters a predominantly male space, or who walks past a particular group of men, will know exactly what I'm talking about. Black women who encounter certain groups of white people, particularly white men, will know exactly what I'm talking about. The hairs stand to attention on the back of your neck. There's a growl in the pit of your stomach that screams, 'Red alert! Shields up!'

The laughter of the boys behind me was growing louder.

What should I do?

Move? But moving seemed dramatic.

What if they were just three boys being . . . well, boys? If I moved, wouldn't that be rude?

I tried to concentrate on the screen but the boys behind me had my full attention instead. Then the comments started. Comments about Black girls being 'up for it' and 'all looking the same' and much worse. Time to go. I stood up to leave and was immediately pushed back down into my seat by rough hands. Two of the boys, sitting to my left and right in the row behind, grabbed my arms and squeezed hard. I was going nowhere. The boy directly behind me put his hands over my breasts and squeezed harder.

'Get off me,' I cried out, struggling against being held in my seat.

The entire time, the three boys were laughing.

I pulled forward trying to get away from the hands that were now all over me. The two boys holding my arms were also pushing their hands down my jumper.

'GET OFF ME!' I screamed, pulling away as hard as I could.

Others in the huge cinema were beginning to look around now. Roaring with laughter, the boys finally released me. I ran out of the auditorium to the women's toilets off the foyer, the boys' laughter ringing in my ears. I went into a toilet cubicle and bawled. Sobbed my heart out. I felt dirty. Physically sick. And even in the toilets, I couldn't shake the sound of the white boys laughing. When I eventually crept out of the loos, I was afraid they'd be waiting for me, but the blue-carpeted corridor was clear. I didn't know what to do. Shouldn't I tell someone? An usher? Someone in the ticket office? Would anyone believe me? My word against three white boys? Besides, they'd be long gone by now. Wouldn't they? Heading back to the auditorium, I opened the doors and walked up the set of five steps until the film was revealed on the giant screen. I looked around for my assailants, but I couldn't see them. The animated characters on the cinema screen beckoned for me to take a seat and resume watching. But I couldn't face it. I turned around and went home, slow fury burning through me with each step.

Once home, I went to my room, curled up in a ball on my bed and cried some more. But they were angry tears, tears of frustration that I'd been so ineffectual. I tried to reason it out. There were three of them, I was alone. They were older teens; I was only fourteen. But why didn't I immediately move or scream the moment they touched me? I couldn't believe I hadn't wanted to move initially in case it seemed rude. For God's sake! So stupid. From the time my boobs started growing, I'd had to put up with teasing from the males in my family, plus lewd comments from men I didn't know, and now this. I was four-teen. Fourteen. What was wrong with these men? And then there were those males – white and Black – who wouldn't or couldn't take no for an answer. The ones who fell into step to 'chat', then fell behind to hurl abuse when it became obvious that their chat-up lines were failing.

It wasn't the first time I was physically assaulted by a male; it wouldn't be the last. The first time was when I was eleven and travelling home from school by bus. The bus was approaching its last stop and I stood up, along with everyone else, waiting for the bus to come to a halt so we could get off. The man I'd been sitting next to put his hand up my skirt and squeezed my bottom as I stood. I spun around to look at him, but he looked straight ahead, his hands now at his side. And I stared, wondering if I'd maybe imagined the hand on my bum. I hadn't, but the fact that I had that thought even now makes me shake my head. What did I do? I tried to take a step forward so he couldn't do it again and got off the bus as soon as possible. I walked home, cursing the guy with each step and each breath. But on the bus, I did and said nothing. These predatory males made me emotionally mute. They robbed me of my voice.

Another time I was in the WH Smith in Lewisham, browsing the books – naturally! – and minding my own business, when I became aware that I was being watched by a white man with a neatly trimmed salt-and-pepper beard and piercing blue eyes. He had to be fifty at least. I was just fifteen. He wore a trilby hat and a camel-coloured woollen coat, with dark trousers and gleaming black shoes. Feeling uncomfortable, I took a sidestep and picked up a book from the shelves. Any book. The man moved closer, maintaining the half-metre distance between us. The old me would've put the book down and left the shop, but by now I was tired of men dictating my actions and movements. I took a deep breath, braced myself and turned directly to face him.

'Can I help you?' I asked.

The man smiled. 'Is there anything you need?'

'Pardon?'

'Is there anything you need? Anything at all? Because I can get it for you.'

What the . . .?

'I love Black girls,' the guy continued. 'Your skin is so silky soft. So smooth. Like velvet. I had a Black girlfriend of around your age, but she went back to Jamaica.'

'I'm fifteen,' I said, appalled. Revolted.

The man's smile broadened. 'I could get you your own flat,' he said eagerly. 'Would you like that? I could get you jewellery. D'you like jewellery?'

Inside I was screaming. Shrieking. 'Piss off, you old goat!' and similar words slammed inside my mind again and again. There were other customers milling around the shop and, although no one was near enough to overhear us, I still felt the need to be polite.

'No, thank you.'

'Let me take you out to dinner. We can discuss it if you'd like.'

I set my facial expression on shoot-to-kill. 'No. Thank. You.'

'Let me look after you,' the man persisted.

After throwing him a furious look, I turned and left the shop. I spent the first five minutes checking to make sure I wasn't being followed. As I walked home, I grew more and more angry. The guy who had put his hand up my skirt when I was only eleven. The boys in the cinema. The weasel in WH Smith who thought it was OK to proposition a fifteen-year-old. Just remembering the way his eyes lit up when I told him my age made me want to projectile-vomit. Forbidden swear words filled my head and filled my mouth, spilling out in enraged whispers. God knows what I must've looked like as I walked, muttering furiously to myself. What was it with men? Was this common practice for white men? Did they just assume that all Black girls were theirs for the taking or could be propositioned in that way? Or was this a global male thing, the innate or nurtured belief in entitlement to women's bodies? By the time I got home I was steaming. I made myself a promise that that would be the last time any man, anywhere, would treat me like a sex object.

In my late teens and into my early twenties I went clubbing regularly, usually with my sister Wendy. I loved nightclubs, dancing and good music, plus – it was great exercise. Once, at the age of eighteen, I met a guy who was charm personified in a nightclub in Ealing. He was great looking with dark-brown eyes, full lips and a gorgeous smile. He was funny, intelligent and laughed at my jokes; I thought I'd found a keeper. We danced together all night until it was time for me to leave.

'Can I meet you again?' he said.

Yes! I'd been hoping he'd ask me that. 'Of course,' I smiled.

'Next Saturday at Mile End Station?' he suggested. 'We could go for a meal together.'

'I'd love to,' I said. And I meant it. 'What time?'

'Six o'clock?'

'It's a date!' My smile was beaming like a lighthouse by now.

Great! I was going to see him again. I really did like him. But then he grabbed my arm, hard, and squeezed harder. It bloody hurt.

'You will turn up, right?'

I plastered a smile on my face, masking the unexpected fear that bloomed in my gut. 'Of course.'

I tried to pull away. His grip grew tighter, his fingers digging into my skin like a series of blunt injections.

'You'll be there?' he asked.

'I'm looking forward to it.' My smile felt brittle, like it was about to crack into a million pieces.

Finally he let me go. 'I'll see you next Saturday,' he smiled. I nodded.

'What's your phone number?' he asked.

Quickly I made one up. He took out a pen and wrote it on the back of his hand. One last smile and I turned to leave the club.

'What did you say your number was again?' he said, grabbing my hand to ask.

I repeated the number. There was nothing wrong with my short-term memory. He checked the numbers I reeled off against the ones on the back of his hand. They were a match. He let go of my hand, his returning smile a switch to turn the charm back on. Much too little, far too late. I'd seen the real man behind the mask. I walked out of the club with my sister and we headed home. The following Saturday came and went and I made sure I was nowhere near Mile End Station. I'd had every intention of turning up until he grabbed my arm. But a man who could deliberately hurt me because I might not turn up to a first date, could and would do a lot worse to me once we became an item.

For weeks and months after the assault in the cinema, I was wary around men and teen boys in particular. So much so, that if I saw a group of teenage boys, I'd cross the road rather than walk through or by them. It took a long time for that to change. As I grew older and my boobs grew bigger, catcalls and explicit suggestions from men were commonplace.

'Come on, darling, show us your tits.'

'Smile, darling. Come over here, I've got something to make you smile.'

'I've got something for you to wrap your lips around.'

On and on. And. On. AND ON it went. It filled me with rage

until I just wanted to scream at the catcallers and the men with obscene suggestions and the boys in the cinema who assaulted me, 'FUCK. YOU. Fuck all of you who think that's an acceptable way to behave.'

To cope, I donned a set of mental armour. I grew harder and colder. No more ready smiles for people in the street, especially men. No more soft expressions to invite conversation. I cultivated a resting bad-bitch face. Medusa had nothing on me. I went into survival mode. It was necessary if I wanted to be left alone. The girl who was interested and curious about people and who would happily chat with complete strangers became buried somewhere deep inside. A girl with a diamond-hard expression and icy-cold demeanour took her place. That demeanour was my sword and shield. I told myself I would no longer be a victim. It makes me sad to look back at myself as an angry teenager, but you do what you have to do to survive. The only superpower I could cultivate to be left alone by predatory men was to nurture an attitude.

And it worked. Sometimes.

Later on, when I became an author, if ever I was asked 'Are you in any of your books?' I would say no – until I wrote *Noughts and Crosses*. Callum as a teenager was straightforward to write because I was writing myself at that age. That need to bury your true self to survive, simmering anger as the default emotion and the assumption that all strangers were enemies, not friends, until proven otherwise – they were all states of being easy to evoke on the page.

Part of the reason I wanted to write stories was to lose myself in the characters I created. Writing fiction was a way to cram many lives and experiences into one lifetime. What I got wrong in real life, I could try to get right through the characters in my books. I could explore the feeling of being a misfit via Vicky in my first novel, *Hacker*. My novel *Tell Me No Lies* was a means to delve into the corrosive effect of secrets. Certain characters became a kind of safety valve, a way to explore not just facets of my past but also facets of my nature. I hasten to add that a number of my characters are pure figments of imagination and are not based on anyone specific, especially not myself. But I've always found creating characters to inhabit particular stories a therapeutic exercise.

The fact that they weren't me and I wasn't them added an extra layer of protection. I could feel for them without bleeding for them. Mostly. Until I created Callum in *Noughts and Crosses*. He was me and I was him, and it made the story gut-wrenching to write – but also unexpectedly cathartic. I discovered that aspects of my past that I thought I'd let go of had merely been buried deep within me. Writing the *Noughts and Crosses* series gave me a way to deal with the past. Before the first of those books, I'd pour my emotions into my characters, but it was easy to step away at the end of each story. To step over them and keep moving. I found it more difficult to let go with the series. My original idea of one book to tell Callum's and Sephy's story turned out to be a twenty-year, six-book and three-novella saga. It's just as well I didn't know that going in.

Decades later, I tried watching Disney's *Robin Hood* again – but I couldn't. I just couldn't. Watching it brought memories of the assault flooding back. It was as if the years had rolled away and I was back in the cinema experiencing the humiliation, the pain, the tears and the boys' laughter.

I have never been able to watch that film.

I know now I never will.

15

After the incident at the cinema, I brooded for days and weeks. I tried to put it out of my mind, but it didn't take much for what had happened to pierce through my defences. A TV programme or a comment overheard would bring it all back – the helplessness, the misplaced shame, the intense outrage and burning anger. It made me think about how my sister and I were expected to do the washing up, the ironing and the cleaning around our house, but that was never asked or expected of my brothers. Was that the same in every household? If so, was that partly what fuelled the sense of entitlement in so many men from such a young age? The unspoken, almost subconscious view that women were put on this Earth to service them and their needs?

My mum had to leave school at fourteen even though she longed to continue, but her brother was encouraged to stay. His education was deemed an investment. My mum's wasn't. She was apprenticed to a seamstress instead. When doing my classical civilisation A level, I found out, to my intense surprise, that my mum had already studied the *Iliad* and the *Odyssey* at school in Barbados. That's when she told me about not being allowed to stay on because she was a girl. As a result, so many avenues were denied to her. I felt terrible for Mum. And I was determined not to take my education or any of my courses for granted.

There were and still are too many children and teenagers in this world who long to go to school and just don't get the

chance. Being denied an education – that closing down of ambition and *potential* – was something I explored when creating
Jude's character in the *Noughts and Crosses* series. He admits
in a moment of rage that he'd longed to stay on at school and
take the opportunity to become someone, instead of working in a dead-end job for the rest of his life. It's partly why Jude
embraces terrorism as a method of societal change, at least in
the beginning. Throughout the *Noughts and Crosses* series, Jude's
acts of terrorism become reduced to a way of expressing his
hatred of Crosses.

When I was a teen and struggling to express myself, I'd write
out all the pain and anger, all the joy and wonder I was feeling
at the time. Sometimes it worked. Sometimes it didn't. I had to
write it out or it felt like I would explode, pop like a balloon too
full of irrepressible emotion. After the incident at the cinema, I
went home and let my fury run riot over the pages of my journal. It was a way of letting my anger burn and then, if not burn
itself out, at least die down a little. Writing my truth became an
essential way of dealing with my thoughts and feelings when
they threatened to overwhelm me.

Sometimes the words would drag me so hard that I struggled to write them all down fast enough. Sometimes it was the
other way round, and I would sit staring at blank pages in my
journal, willing myself to have courage enough to fill them
with my true emotions. Doing so was scary at first, but it soon
became an outlet. A way to make sense of myself and my reality, a way to release the tension I felt inside. No wonder then that
I filled so many diaries and journals in my teenage years! Writing had become necessary for maintaining any kind of equilib-
rium regarding my mental health.

Writing saved me.

16

At sixteen, I had my school, libraries, reading and a desire to get a decent education. I was determined to make something of my life. I just didn't have a clue what that something would be. I had a serious decision to make – whether or not to stay on at school. In an ideal world, I wanted to stay and study for my A levels. But an ideal world was outside my solar system. Our house in Lewisham was several miles away from my school in Peckham and things were so bad financially that I didn't even know how I'd find the bus fare to get to school, never mind how I'd be able to buy all the books I needed. The money I'd make from my summer holiday job wasn't going to be enough to get me through two years of sixth form.

The end of the summer term was fast approaching and my school was pushing me for a decision as to whether I'd be staying on. All my friends would be – it wasn't even a question for them.

I racked and cracked my brains trying to come up with a solution, but even if I worked throughout the summer holiday, that would only fund one term of school, two at the very most. Higher education was beginning to look more and more unobtainable.

Just when I'd resigned myself to leaving school for good, I received a letter telling me that I was eligible for the equivalent of an Education Maintenance Allowance. The letter stated I was entitled to receive £122 per term to help me with my education. It felt as though God had delivered the letter personally. All the thoughts I'd had of working in a department store or trying to get an office job weren't just put on a back burner – they were taken off the stove altogether. With that kind of money, I could stay on at school. The weight I'd carried for so long was lifted and I swear it felt like I was floating. I selected the A levels I wanted to pursue in the sixth form – chemistry, geology and classical civilisation – and I was all set.

I picked subjects that I thought would help me to get a decent job when I left school. It was a coin toss between classical civilisation and English literature, but the books I'd studied for my English lit O level had been so dry that studying more dusty tomes didn't really appeal, whereas learning about classical civilisations – their culture, religions, mythologies and languages – did.

I spent the summer working at the BT telephone exchange and then I was back at school, determined not to miss a single day. But on the very first day of term, I was informed that geology wasn't going to go ahead; I'd been the only one to enrol for it at A level and the school wasn't going to lay on a teacher just for me. How could I be the only one? Was there no one else in the sixth form interested in the structure and composition of the Earth? Whenever I visited a beach, I lost track of time analysing interesting rocks, examining their strata and investigating their composition. I'd memorised the Mohs scale of hardness and applied it to each new rock and gem I handled. I couldn't care less about the monetary value of diamonds; I loved the molecular structure of them! Was there no one else in the school who loved petrology, mineralogy and palaeontology the way I did? Apparently not. Bye, bye, geology.

So now I was down to two A levels – chemistry and classical civilisation.

Three weeks into my chemistry A-level course, I realised I'd made a huge mistake. I loved chemistry. I loved all the sciences (physics the least, admittedly). The trouble was, apart from biology, I had no natural aptitude for them. Chemistry A level was full of maths and I was already struggling. I didn't need a crystal ball to tell me that over the next two years, my struggles would get harder. Much harder. After a chat with Miss Brace, the A-level English teacher, where I learned what books would need to be studied for the course, I switched from chemistry to English literature. And thank you, Jesus, that I did! I'd missed four weeks of English classes, mostly work on Chaucer's *Troilus and Criseyde* and Shakespeare's *Othello*.

When I started reading *Othello*, a surprised thrill ran through me when I realised that Othello was *Black*. Ohmigod! A character in a play – a Shakespeare play, no less – was Black. Until now, I had never, not once, read anything – book, play, comic, pamphlet – that featured a Black main character. I was supposed to read up to Act 3 to catch up with everyone else in my class. I spent the weekend reading the entire play – every action, every speech, every line, every word.

Unless you've been in the same boat, it's hard to imagine what it's like to love a world from which you feel permanently excluded. That was me and the world of books and literature – until *Othello*. Yes, Othello was an arse and all he did was sit and speak to his wife about the wandering hankie, but he was newly married and, more importantly, newly in love. I excused his foolishness because, damn, here was a Black man in a Shakespeare play.

By the end of that weekend, I knew I'd made the right decision regarding swapping chemistry for English. After we'd finished with *Othello* and I had sucked the bones of the play clean, we moved on to Shakespeare's *Troilus and Cressida*. I found that play far less engaging, but we were studying it to do a compare and contrast with Chaucer's version of the same story.

Miss Brace was a wonderful teacher who really knew her subject and brought the lessons to life. She also encouraged us to go to the theatre as often as we could, and arranged to take us at least once a term. She freely admitted that she hated children – especially the younger ones – but she loved teaching English! During one particularly long, slow-moving lesson, as we were analysing a scene from *Troilus and Cressida*, Miss Brace said, 'I'm sure Shakespeare had a dose of the clap when he wrote this play. It's so misogynistic!'

My jaw hit the floor – and mine wasn't the only one. In a classroom full of seventeen-year-old girls, I don't think there was one of us who wasn't shocked. We glanced at each other, wondering if we'd heard right. Had Miss Brace really said that she believed Shakespeare had an STI when he wrote the play we were reading? Miss Brace, meanwhile, had moved on to discuss Pandarus's motivations, but there was a twinkle in her eyes and a slight smile on her lips.

But a light bulb had switched on in my head. Shakespeare was a real person and not some super-being who roamed the galaxy and accidentally fell to Earth. He wasn't a god or born an icon. He farted and peed and belched and loved and laughed and got angry and suffered despair and pulled on his pantaloons one leg at a time the same as every other human on the planet. He was a person. Talented, but a person nonetheless, the same as Dickens, Martin Luther King, Muhammad Ali, Rosa Parks and a host of other people I admired. The same as Jane Austen, the Brontës and Daphne du Maurier. They were people who did great things but who, I'd bet, also got a lot of things wrong in their lives. It was a strangely comforting thought.

Maybe there were no heroes, just people who stepped up and did what needed to be done. Maybe it was simply a question of being in the right place at the right time. Good timing? Guardian angel placement? Who knew? Not me. But these people, all these special people, were human first and human last. And if they could do something with their lives, in some cases against all the odds, then why couldn't I?

But do what?

I was studying for two A levels at school – English literature and classical civilisation – but had too much free time on my hands and was getting bored. As Lewisham College was within walking distance of my house, I headed up there one day to see what A-level courses they ran that weren't available at school. And I found what seemed like the perfect one for me – sociology. The course description called sociology the study of the development, structure and collective behaviours and interactions of human society. It offered the tools to analyse society and the place of the individual within it. Excellent! So I enrolled on the A-level sociology course – and loved it. All my courses required a great deal of reading but I didn't mind. Sociology was so interesting. And when my form teacher found out that I was studying for an extra A level outside of school, she said that I could take the exam at school rather than at the college. That way I wouldn't have to pay to take the exam.

The more I thought about what I might do when I left school, the more an idea I'd had in primary school started to grow and blossom. From the time I was eight or nine, I'd had only one career in mind – to be an English teacher. A love of stories – of words, their shape on a page, their feel and taste on my tongue, the images they painted in my head – had shaped my thinking. It made sense that they should shape my life.

A teacher.

I could be an English teacher. That was it! An idea that had faded slightly, now bloomed again like a summer rose. I loved my English literature lessons and I'd always dreamed of teaching it, so: hell yes!

An English teacher.

It was what I was born to do.

I started looking into English courses at university and found the perfect one for me. English and Drama at Goldsmiths College in London. I hadn't initially considered doing drama as part of my degree. The thought of standing up in front of an audience and speaking was enough to leave me in a cold sweat. In the handful of school drama productions I'd joined, I was given roles like Third Soldier from the Left, which, quite frankly, were right at my level. But here was a chance to discover my inner actress. To embrace the dramatic. To become a new me by inhabiting the skin of different people and living their lives, even if just for a while, on stage. The more I thought about it, the sweeter the idea grew. Plus, the fact that Goldsmiths was just a bus ride away from home greatly appealed.

Mrs T, a biology teacher and the sixth-form careers advisor, scheduled an individual meeting with each student to discuss our plans for the future. It was Mrs T who wrote our references on our Universities Central Council on Admissions (UCCA) forms – so this meeting wasn't just a formality; it was crucial. On the day of my appointment, I was all excitement. I had my future figured out. I was *born* to be an English teacher. I walked into Mrs T's tiny office and settled myself in the chair she indicated.

Getting straight down to it, Mrs T asked with a smile, 'So what is it that you want to do when you leave school, Lorie?'

I had my answer prepared. 'I want to go to Goldsmiths College to do an English and Drama degree and after that I want to become an English teacher.'

Mrs T frowned. Her frown deepened as my eager smile began

to fade. 'Oh no. Black people don't become teachers. Why don't you be a secretary instead?'

My mouth fell open. I stared at her. I couldn't've been more shocked if she'd gut-punched me.

'Besides,' she added hastily when she saw the look on my face. 'I don't think you'll pass your English A level so I can't give you a good reference.'

'I've never failed an English exam in my life,' I protested.

'Teaching isn't for the likes of you,' she insisted. 'I tell you what, why don't you go to a polytechnic and study something like Business Studies?'

I barely heard what she said next. Her mouth was still moving but my mind was full of silent protestations. Not pass my English A level? What the hell? Where did she get that from? Was that something Miss Brace had told her? Did my teacher expect me to fail my A-level exam? I didn't believe it. Miss Brace had given me top grades for my homework and had told me that my work was excellent. Or was she someone who would say one thing to my face and another behind my back? No! No way. Miss Brace wasn't like that, and she'd have no qualms telling me to get it together if I was slacking. No, this was all from Mrs T, who spoke with such conviction, such authority that for a moment I wondered what she knew that I didn't. Not pass my English exam? Bollocks to that.

'I'll show you, you old cow,' I thought furiously. Yet despair and, for the first time, doubt sprung up like poisonous weeds inside me.

'Business Studies at a poly would suit you much better. That's what my son is doing,' Mrs T added with a smile.

I couldn't care less what her son was or wasn't doing. She carried on talking but I hardly heard her. I was still stuck on what she'd previously said.

Not pass my English A level?
We'd just see about that.

But what could I do about going to university? Without a good reference no university would take me, and Mrs T had already told me she wouldn't provide one. I'd never failed an English exam in my life. I never got less than a B. Why would she think that? Why would she say that? Because I'd dared to dream of being a teacher? Because I had ideas above my station, my class, my skin colour – or all of the above?

My dream of being a teacher got shot full of holes and bit the dust.

Mrs T handed me prospectuses from four polytechnics and sent me on my way. We had very little to say to each other after that. One conversation had derailed my future. Feeling I had no choice, I applied to do Business Studies at three of the four polytechnics Mrs T had recommended and got into all of them. But even before I sat my A-level exams, I knew Business Studies would be a huge mistake. I consoled myself with the thought that the course would be better than nothing. Its structure was broad enough that I could apply for a range of jobs afterwards. My life was heading down an unknown path.

I got the required grades and decided on Huddersfield Polytechnic. I'd never been to Huddersfield, so before accepting I travelled up by train to check it out, and I liked the look of the Yorkshire countryside. That was my main reason for choosing Huddersfield. If I was going to spend three years studying a subject that didn't interest me, I might as well do so where scenic surroundings were a mere bus ride away.

That was the last time I let someone else make a major life decision for me.

17

September 1980. I was embarking on my very own adventure. This would be the longest I'd ever been away from home and I was so ready for it. No more having to explain what time I'd be back and why. No more having to explain what I'd bought and why. No more having to share my own place and space. Here I was in Huddersfield, in my very own room in a hall of residence. Our floor of ten rooms contained only women. Each floor alternated between men and women. There was only one bathroom per floor at the end of each corridor, with a kitchen opposite. My room, my very own room, consisted of a single bed pushed against one wall and a desk against the opposite wall with a single shelf above it. A narrow chair was pushed to sit neatly under the desk. If I stood in the middle of the room and lifted my arms thirty-five degrees away from my sides, I would touch the chair and the bed with either hand. There was a tiny pinewood-coloured wardrobe next to the desk. And that was it. But I loved it!

On the first day at my new home, all the women on the floor left their doors open so that we could buzz in and out of each other's rooms to introduce ourselves. Here it was, my new start, my chance to remake myself as someone I would want to hang around with. It felt as though I'd spent my teen years in a perpetual motion of making and remaking myself into some nebulous image that was always just out of reach. An image which, at the time, was an amalgam of others' expectations butting heads with my own.

I was delighted to discover that directly opposite me was another Black girl, Lorraine from Birmingham. We were two Black girls far away from home, in a strange environment to be carefully navigated – and we immediately became friends. That's what we do as Black women in new, unfamiliar spaces where we are few in number – we navigate. We gauge expressions, moods, words, voices, atmospheres – all the things that represent a thin line between relative calm and imminent danger. There is a certain smile that passes between Black people in mostly white spaces. A smile of acknowledgement, of recognition, of understanding.

A smile that says, 'I see you.'

So it was with me and Lorraine. Although we were on different courses, we cooked and went to nightclubs together. The nearest decent club was almost two miles away from our halls. But so what? Lacking funds, we would take a bus there and walk home at two in the morning, singing all the good songs we'd heard that night.

During freshers' week, I blitzed through the assembly hall filled with tables advertising the different polytechnic student societies. Drama and dance, art and law, hockey and various sports and a host of other hobbies, pastimes and subjects. Excitement burst from me with open, grasping, clasping hands. I wanted to learn everything, join them all. I stopped at the skiing table.

'Where d'you go skiing?' I asked.

'There's a dry-slope skiing centre in Harrogate. Sign up and come with us,' smiled the white guy with kind, welcoming brown eyes behind round glasses seated at the sign-up-for-skiing table. 'We provide a coach to take us there once a fortnight.'

Skiing owed me an experience. I signed up.

When the day came, I hopped on the organised coach, my smile wide, my mind open. On arrival at the dry-ski slope, my smile fell slightly. The 'snow' consisted of flat, white plastic doughnuts ringed with short, bendy plastic tendrils. It wasn't snow, but it *was* skiing. It would be enough. I was given skis and boots. When I heard we'd be skiing on dry slopes, I'd assumed a certain warmth to the skiing facilities. My mistake. It was bloody freezing. I didn't mind. It meant I was closer to the real-life experience I'd missed back in Year 9. I joined the beginners' class, learning how to start and stop. I skied about three metres, then worked my way back up to our starting positions. Down and up. Down and up. I fell once, my knee making contact with the concrete beneath the plastic rings. And it hurt. Wincing, I got to my feet and examined my knee. Yep, it was bleeding. I brushed it off and walked crab-like up the slope to join the back of the queue. The instructor glanced at my knee and insisted I head down to the reception for a plaster to cover it. 'Big fuss about nothing,' I thought.

In Huddersfield, I wasn't a wimp. I wasn't the girl who got teased for being too weak to stand up straight with my knees locked. This was a brand-new me. And the brand-new me didn't cry or wimp out or back down. The brand-new me was *fierce*. Fearless. I loved the brand-new me. I had also signed up for kung fu lessons and attended every Wednesday evening without fail. I loved them – the rigour, the discipline. Choosing kung fu was taking back power into my own hands. There would be no more men groping, pinching, sliding their hands up my skirt or down my blouse. There would be no more pre-planning and navigating routes as if I were prey among predators.

Halfway through the first term, I took stock. I loved Huddersfield and my new social life, I loved my kung fu lessons and dry-slope skiing. Everything was perfect – except my course.

BA Business Studies was boring as hell. Surprise, surprise! The economics lectures left me asleep with my eyes open. Accounting gave me a headache, and as for maths and stats? Well, the lecturer might as well have been speaking Martian. Marketing flowed over me like shower water. The only subject that made any kind of impression and that I thought was interesting was business law. And I was good at it. But one module out of however many wasn't enough to pass my end-of-year exams, and if I didn't pass every subject, I'd be out. I had to face facts. Business Studies was not for me and I needed to find another course quick, fast and in a hurry if I was to stand any chance of staying.

The other vulture picking at my flesh was money: I was close to stony broke. Again. Barely halfway through the first term and I had enough money to last me one week, maybe two if I lived on beans. No toast. My polytechnic tuition fees as well as my rent were being paid for by the government, but the grant payments were made at the start of each term and having so much money in my bank account had gone to my head. I withdrew money like I thought it was never-ending, and that money burned holes straight through my pockets. There was no point in phoning Mum to ask for more as I knew she didn't have any to spare. I'd never had an allowance before and had no clue how to budget and pace my spending. Being homeless and sustaining yourself from day to day or week to week didn't allow for long-term financial planning. Now that lack of knowledge was biting chunks out of my butt.

But today was Wednesday. Kung fu day – so all other worries would have to wait until my lesson was over. And at least my lessons were paid for until the end of term. One of the things I loved about kung fu was the total focus required during the class; the attention on my core, my posture, the concentration needed for the punches and kicks to explode from me in disciplined, if amateur, control. Anything less could cause injuries. The sensei would walk up and down the rows of students, straightening a wrist here, adjusting a stance there. He paused before me as I punched the air at his command. A nod and he moved on. And I felt good. He had found no need to correct anything. I was where I was meant to be. But halfway through the lesson, something went very wrong. My stomach began to hurt in a way I'd never experienced before.

18

As I worked through the kata, the pain that started in my stomach slithered all the way around my waist and gripped like a python. Its squeeze grew tighter until I could barely stand. With a bow to the sensei, I left the dojo and went to the changing room, where I immediately lay down, clasping my stomach. The pain began to ebb, easing enough for me to get my breath back. I didn't bother with a shower. Grabbing my coat and bag, I headed home. Every time the pain hit it doubled me over, but I finally made it back to my room to collapse on my bed. The iron band around my waist tightened further, now slicing into me. Agony, intense and crippling, clawed at my insides. Relentless. Excruciating. It was like nothing I'd ever felt before. Looking back on that day, I struggle to remember anything else about it. What had I had for breakfast? For lunch? What had I done with my morning, my afternoon? It isn't just a blur, it's a blank. There was the evening kung fu class followed by the slow, fiery squeeze of my insides as the October sun began to set outside my window.

I searched through my desk drawer for some painkillers – aspirin, paracetamol, anything would do. There was nothing. Frustrated, I slammed the drawer shut. Pain dictated that every action, every sound, hurt. Even the light from the single bulb in my room was too bright and stabbed at my eyes. Flinging open my door, I staggered across the hallway to Lorraine's room and banged on her door. It took forever to finally open.

'Lorraine, d'you h-have any aspirin?'

By now the pain was sawing me in half, affecting my voice, stifling my words until they were barely a whisper.

'Lori! Are you all right? No, I'm sorry, I don't have any,' Lorraine said, her eyes growing wider with concern. 'Are you OK?'

I nodded, but the lie was obvious. Hands against the wall, I tried to make it back to my room. Two steps, then I turned, sliding down the wall as my body gave in and gave out and the pain took over completely.

What happened next is a series of images, like snapshots. A scream. People running. Paramedics. I was lifted up. An ambulance. Lights flashing through the windows. Sirens. Even though the pain was ripping through me, I remember thinking, 'I'm in an ambulance. I've never been in an ambulance before. How exciting.' But that thought was fleeting; another tortuous wave washed through me. I was wheeled into hospital. People loomed over me. I was lying on a bed, my head slightly raised, with doctors and nurses bustling around me. The whole time I was in control of nothing.

One of the surgeons standing over me said to his colleague, 'It's unusual to find someone with this disease around here.'

Around here? What was he talking about? *Who* was he talking about? What was going on? I tried to speak but there was something hard in my mouth. I spat it out, glancing down at the rubber bung that hit my chest then rested still.

'What disease? What disease?' I asked.

Eyes popping out of their heads, the doctors and nurses in the room stared at me like I was a ghost who'd suddenly appeared and started talking to them. Looking back, the memory of the shocked faces, the stunned silence in the room, still makes me smile wryly. They obviously thought I'd already been sufficiently anaesthetised. Ironically, it was the intense pain that meant I was still awake.

'We weren't talking about you,' said the other surgeon. 'We were talking about someone else. Another case.'

A quick nod from the first surgeon to someone behind me. A nurse picked up the rubber bung from my chest and pushed it back into my mouth. Glances were exchanged around me.

They're lying.

Even in my spaced-out, semi-sedated state I knew that. I wanted to ask more, but the room began to fade into darkness.

Silence.

Nothing.

The next afternoon I woke up in a hospital bed, wondering what had happened to me. I called out to a nurse, asking exactly that.

'A doctor will be along later to explain everything to you. OK?'

She bustled off before I could reply. My abdomen didn't feel right. I lifted up the blanket and sheet covering me to check my stomach. There was a large square bandage over the right-hand side of my abdomen. I was tempted to take it off to look at what they'd done but I decided to wait until the doctor arrived. However, I couldn't stop coughing. Another nurse came to prop me up so I wasn't lying quite so flat.

'That's the anaesthetic,' she informed me cheerily after I had another coughing fit. 'It'll soon pass.'

Every time I had a coughing spasm, I placed a hand firmly over the bandage on my stomach, afraid my stitches would pop.

Less than an hour later, Lorraine came to visit me. She sat down by my bed and watched as I tried to suppress yet another cough which felt like it would surely rip out my stitches, tearing my abdomen in two.

Lorraine inhaled deeply. 'Lori, they took out your appendix.'

Did they? A doctor had yet to sit down and speak to me about anything. I hadn't had a proper conversation with an actual doctor since I was brought to the hospital. At least that explained the pain I was still feeling in my abdomen – and the stitches.

Lorraine took another deep breath. 'Look, Lori. You do know you've got sickle cell, right?'

I stared at her. 'I've got what?'

'Sickle cell. The doctor told me you have sickle cell.'

What was that? Something I'd barely even heard of. I didn't know what that meant. And how dare they tell Lorraine without telling me first? *How dare they?* What the hell?

Eventually Lorraine left, promising me my friends from my floor would be coming by to see me later. I barely heard her. I lay still, my eyes closed, shell-shocked.

What the hell was sickle cell? Where was the doctor who was supposed to explain everything to me? I had so many questions. So many . . .

That's how I fell asleep.

That's how I woke up.

My eyes still closed, two words laced with shards of glass and rusty nails spun round uncontrollably in my head – sickle cell. I heard voices approaching. They were a bed away. I opened my eyes, only to shut them almost immediately when a male doctor and female nurse moved to stand at the foot of my bed.

'Ah yes,' said the doctor. 'This case is an interesting one.'

'The sickle cell patient?'

'Indeed. She had her appendix removed yesterday. It's a shame about this one. With her sickle cell, she'll be dead by thirty.'

What?

I lay totally still. The pillow beneath my neck had been replaced by a guillotine, and I was waiting for the blade to fall. All I could think was, 'I'm going to die – before I'm thirty years old.' And at eighteen, thirty suddenly didn't seem so far away after all.

My lifespan clock had started ticking.

Maybe that was the moment I developed a loathing for the sound made by clocks and old-fashioned watches. I hate the steady, relentless rhythm of the tick-tock as they count down the hours, the minutes, the moments. It sets my teeth on edge.

In my version of heaven all the clocks have been removed.

My version of hell is a lonely house full of nothing but stairs – and ticking clocks.

Overhearing the doctor and nurse pronounce on my life expectancy was the event that changed the course of my life. When I overheard them, I thought I'd lost my future, that all my long-term goals, plans and ambitions would have to be abandoned. In just over a decade, I wouldn't even be here.

Or so I thought.

For the next several years, I was all about the money. If I was going to die young, then I wanted to earn enough to live life the way I wanted. I joined a computing software house where I met my partner, Neil (more on that later!), I pushed to go on computing evening classes and short courses, I agitated to get more challenging work and was happy to do any overtime required. I worked my way up from glorified filing clerk to systems programmer to project manager. At twenty-one, I bought a two-bedroom flat in Brockley. Opportunities weren't given a chance to pass me by. Instead, they were grabbed and put in a chokehold. My story would take several more unexpected twists in the years that followed, but when I hit my thirties, I suffered another loss.

Perhaps the greatest loss of all.

19

In my early twenties, I made the decision that motherhood was not for me. I didn't want children. The prediction of my remaining lifespan still occupied my thoughts and I decided it would be selfish to bring a child into the world when I wouldn't be around to look after them. In my late twenties that decision mellowed into ambivalence. I liked children, I liked being around them, but maybe motherhood was something that would never happen to me. Que sera sera.

My thirtieth birthday came and went. I didn't die!

By now, I had my dream job. I was an author. And when I hit my thirties, it was as if a new desire now had the space to be born within me. I wanted a child. Where the hell had that come from? What had happened to my indifference? As the months passed, my yearning for a child of my own grew worse, until I couldn't pass a buggy or pram without looking into it. Babies were all I could think about. I drank in their appearance, the look of them, the way they smelled. Every baby's cry was a Marvin Gaye song. I had it bad! Parents and guardians enjoying their time with their children had my full, unadulterated envy. And as for pregnant women, I was jealous of each and every one of them. To hold and nurture a new human being under your heart knowing that in a few months, you'd bring a child into the world was indeed magical. Parents who smacked or screamed at their children got my full ire. Didn't they realise how lucky they were to have a child in the first place?

My partner Neil, bless him, realised how miserable I was at

the prospect of not having a child of our own and agreed to try for one, mainly for my sake. He worried about whether he'd make a good father and was still as ambivalent as I'd been only a couple of years before.

I became pregnant.

To say I was overjoyed would be a gross understatement. I'd been pregnant once before, in my mid-twenties, and all I'd felt then was panic. I reckoned I was far too young to have a child. I'd even looked into the steps I'd have to take to have an abortion, though I wasn't sure I could go through with it. But soon after I discovered I was pregnant, I had a miscarriage. One day I was pregnant, the next day I was bleeding. Chris, as I came to think of my child – Christopher for a boy, Christella for a girl – was no more than four or five weeks old when I lost them. And I'm not going to lie – mixed in with the wistful regret was a tinge of relief because I truly felt that I wasn't ready.

When I became pregnant the second time, I thought I had it made. It was all happening just as I wanted. Life couldn't get any better. When I was fourteen weeks pregnant and feeling sure that nothing could happen to my baby now, I told my mum. I told everyone. I was elated and wanted to share the news far and wide.

But then it all went wrong.

20

Tara,
I think of you.
Not every day
Not even every other day,
But I do think of you.
Often.

You were so wanted
So loved
When you were still
Just a dot inside me.

I couldn't wait to meet you,
Greet you,
Hold you
Hug you,
Lift you
Love you.

During my first ultrasound
We found out you were a girl.
We named you Tara
After the Kensington hotel
Where you were conceived.

Lucky we weren't in a Ramada,
Or a Malmaison.
Or a Premier Inn.

I wanted to meet you
and greet you
and hold you
and hug you
and lift you
and love you
so much.
So, so much.

Every day I spoke to you,
sang to you.
Tara, we were both so ready for you
to be a part of our lives.
And I was so overjoyed
I couldn't keep my mouth shut.
I told my mum, my sister,
I told everyone
that you were on your way,
You were coming.

But at fourteen weeks pregnant,
peeing became a problem.
The stream went from
Niagara,
to summer rainfall
to misty drizzle
to nothing.

So I went to Lewisham Hospital.
'Why can't I pee?'
A doctor told me
I'd need a catheter.
Then I'd be as right as rain.
'But why have I stopped peeing?'
'Just one of those things,' said the doctor.

He left it to a nurse,
A white woman of about my height,
her blonde hair tied back in a ponytail,
to insert the catheter.

She tried to insert it.
'Ow!'
She withdrew and tried again.
'Ow!'
She withdrew, gave me a look
And RAMMED it into me.
Crammed it into me.
A bayonet
Straight and true
Jammed inside of me.

Like I was an animal.
A vet with a pet
Wouldn't be so cruel.

And the pain . . .
Oh Lord, the pain . . .
A judder jolted me
A shudder shot through me

A chill, cold and cruel,
that ran into my bones
and settled there.

'It's in,' said the nurse.
And she bustled away.
And that was the moment you died, Tara.
That was the moment.
You died.

Only at that time
I didn't know it.
All I knew was the pain
and confusion
of being a victim
of a nurse in a hurry.
A nurse who couldn't
or wouldn't
view me as a human being
worthy of kindness and care.

Bladder empty,
My husband took me home.
But I didn't feel right.
Something was wrong.
I just didn't know what.

Just over twenty-four hours later,
Early on a Monday morning,
I started to bleed.
A spit,
A spot,

But it wouldn't stop.
My husband was at work,
I was alone.
What should I do?
I started to cramp up
Like a bad period pain.
And I knew,
I instinctively knew
What was happening.

I begged you, Tara,
To hold on
Until I could get help.
I slipped on some shoes
And a jacket
And walked to the hospital.
I didn't phone for an ambulance,
I figured it would be faster to walk,
And I wanted to get there as soon as possible
So that they could stop the bleeding
And save you, Tara.

I got to the A&E reception
And said, 'I think I'm having a miscarriage.'
I was immediately seen.
'Please. Please . . .' I silently begged.
'Please . . . Please,' I openly said.
But it was too late.
You had already gone.
You'd died over twenty-four hours before
When a catheter was thrust into me
In a violation
That cost your life.

'I'm sorry,' said another white nurse,
A brunette with sympathetic eyes,
As the spit, the spot
Turned into a river.
'She's gone.'
'NO!' I cried out,
Like a wounded animal.
Like the animal
The blonde nurse
From twenty-four hours before
Obviously thought I was.
'I'm so sorry,' said the sympathetic eyes.
She left the cubicle,
Drawing the curtains
As I cried and cried.

At fourteen weeks pregnant
You were so real to me, Tara.
I was planning for your first steps,
Your first words,
Your first period,
Your first kiss,
Your first steady partner,
Your wedding.
I was anticipating it all.

But you were gone.

Neil arrived less than one hour later.
'How did you get here so fast?'
I sniffed through tears.
'The nurse phoned me and
told me what was happening,

So I left work,' he said.
'Just like that?'
'Of course like that.'
'Didn't they mind?'
'I don't give a shit.'
And he hugged me
And held me
And we both mourned
The loss of our daughter –
Tara.
And I couldn't stop crying.

They asked me if I wanted to see you.
How could I look at my dead daughter?
How would I cope with that?
'I think you should,' said Neil.
'I think you should,' said the brunette nurse.

I reluctantly agreed.
They brought you to me.
And you were so small
And yet so big.
About the size
Of my index finger
And so perfectly formed.

My baby, Tara.
I looked at you
And the tears lessened
Because here you were
Real.
My daughter, Tara.

You were real.
And though you hadn't lived,
I was still your mum.

Seeing you
Brought me a strange kind of calm
Which I hadn't anticipated.

Seeing you
Brought me a strange kind of peace
Which I didn't expect.

Seeing you
Brought it home
How much I loved you,
And just how much I *hated* the nurse
Who had taken you away from me.

The nurses told me
As I waited for my D&C
– dilation and curettage –
To scrape the last traces of you
From my womb and
        out of my body,
That I could see you at any time,
All I had to do was ask.

I did ask,
Just once more.
You were lying on a bed of cotton wool
In a small plastic container.

And it did help
To see you again,
One last time.
To say
a proper goodbye.

Mum came to visit me
When I was about to be taken to theatre
for my D&C.
I'd only just said
a final farewell,
And I couldn't stop weeping,
for what I'd had
and what I'd lost.
I didn't want Mum to see me
distraught.
I didn't want her
to worry,
be sad,
feel bad.
'I'm sorry, Mum.'
I tried to wipe away the tears
punctuating the inane words of apology,
But they had
A will of their own.
'I'll be all right, Mum,
Please don't worry.'
I took her hand in mine,
And she burst into tears
at the sight of my own.
'Don't cry, Mum,
I'll be OK,' I said.

'Please don't cry.'
Mum was mortified,
At crying in front of me.
I could see she was trying not to,
But sometimes
Grief spills from one vessel
To the next
To the next
Relentlessly.

After my D&C,
To scrape every trace of you
And your existence
Out of my body,
I was sent home.

The next year was spent in a haze of
Trying to work
And bursting into tears.
Trying to write
And being overwhelmed with despair.
Trying to live
And wanting my baby,
My Tara.

There were days
When I'd phone Neil
And just say,
'Can you come home?'
And he'd drop everything,
Meetings and greetings,
Deadlines and dealings,

And come home
Just to hold me
As I cried.

At first, I couldn't think of you, Tara,
Without tears in my eyes,
But after a while, I could think of you
With pain in my heart
But it wouldn't be quite so pin-sharp
Not quite so . . . lacerating.

And after a longer while
I could consider you
With wistful sadness.

I still wonder about you;
On days of joy or sorrow
I wonder about you.
Your looks
Your height
Your likes
Your loves
Who and what
You would've been
Could've been.
I still wonder about you.

And as for the blonde nurse,
Who took you from me,
I think about her too.
Best believe, I do.

21

By the time I became pregnant with Tara, my career as a writer had started and I had six or seven books under my belt. After Tara's death, it took me a long time to get my head back in the writing game. Hell, it took me a long time to get my head back into anything at all. Well over a year. Neil was always there when I needed him but I was living a life deferred. I was too lost in grief to take much notice of anything around me, including Neil. I'm ashamed to admit that it took too long to appreciate just how much he was grieving too.

And as for work? Oh, I'd write a page of this, a bit of that, but my focus was hibernating, waiting for the grief inside to . . . not disappear, exactly, but lessen. It took a while before I could think of Tara without tears pricking my eyes, but the day did come. One of the biggest revelations about having a miscarriage was learning just how many of my female friends and colleagues had gone through the same thing – and in a number of cases, more than once. Miscarriages seemed to be a topic that was off-limits between women unless and until it was brought up by someone who had gone through it. But knowing I was not alone in what had happened to me and the grief I felt afterwards did actually help. I listened as other women shared the steps they'd had to take to move on. I learned that there was no hard-and-fast rule for when the grief would pass, but that it did pass, or at least became more bearable, more manageable.

Years later, after I'd finally had my daughter Liz, one friend I got to know while waiting to collect my daughter each day from school told me she'd had eleven miscarriages. *Eleven*. When we met she had two beautiful daughters, but I can imagine only too well the years of heartache she had to navigate to get to that point. To this day she has my admiration for not giving up after each heartbreak. I can't help wondering if I would've persevered for that long – the honest answer is that I simply don't know.

I do know that the pain of losing Tara didn't take away my longing for a child and my desire to keep trying. A couple of years later we were blessed with our daughter Liz. When I was pregnant with Liz, I told no one until I was twenty weeks pregnant. And even then, I spent my pregnancy in a state of high anxiety, worried that I might lose this baby too. But it was worth it. At around thirty weeks, I began to dare to think of names for our forthcoming child.

All kinds of different and wonderful names popped into my head. In the running? Shayne, Splendid, Demerara, Autumn, Luna, River, Moon, Sunshine, Star. Nature was a definite theme.

Neil put his foot down. 'For God's sake! For a pop star's or actor's child, then maybe,' he replied to my every suggestion. 'But our daughter is the one who'll have to live with it, not you.'

When at last our daughter was born, gave her first cry and opened her eyes to look at me as I held her close, the nurse asked, 'What's her name?'

Without hesitation and to my surprise, I replied, 'Elizabeth.' Now where did that come from?

Whenever the subject of proposed baby names is mentioned at the family dinner table, my daughter always turns to Neil and says a heartfelt, 'Thank you, Dad.' Most of the names that were in the running she hates with a passion. Funny thing is, she doesn't much like the name Elizabeth either. Ah well!

22

Things I Lost

Beloved comics
Books I cherished
Childhood dolls
Plants that perished
Christmas treats
Birthday toys
Music playing
Joyous noise
Peace and a sanctuary
A bolthole, a home
A sense of security
A place of my own
A belief in others
To keep me protected
Innocence and trust,
And the belief,
The hopeful belief,
The erroneous belief,
I'd never be rejected.

Loss.

Anger

23

Ah, anger!

Anger gets shit done! I've found anger to be a great motivator and, when used constructively, an irresistible driving force. Here's the thing. As a Black woman, I have to be careful how I channel my anger and even more careful how I express it. There are those all too ready to stamp 'ANGRY BLACK WOMAN' on my forehead. It's a lazy, ignorant, incorrect stereotype all too often ascribed to Black women who speak up for themselves. It's also used as an excuse to dismiss us and not listen to what we're saying. Stories are my way of using my voice – sometimes the words spring from anger, sometimes from laughter, sometimes from sadness, but most often from love.

As Maya Angelou stated, 'You should be angry. So use that anger. You write it. You paint it. You dance it. You march it. You vote it. You do everything about it. You talk it. Never stop talking it.'

Amen.

24

In 1980, when I was rushed to Huddersfield Infirmary, I learned after my operation that the surgeons thought I was suffering from a burst appendix. There wasn't a damned thing wrong with my appendix but, seeing as they were in the vicinity, they whipped it out anyway. When a doctor did finally speak to me after my operation, he told me I had, quote, bowel adhesions and tangled intestines. Pure bullshit, of course. What I'd had was a misdiagnosed sickle cell crisis. I confirmed this years later when, back in hospital due to yet another crisis, a nurse accidentally left the thick folder containing my medical notes at the bottom of my bed and I read them from start to finish.

Back in 1980 in Huddersfield, I was told what I had by Lorraine, the diagnosis was confirmed by a nurse, briefly addressed by a doctor and then I was sent on my merry way. The doctors didn't tell me anything because they didn't have anything to tell me. They didn't have a clue. I had been opened up for nothing, stitched back together and sent home. After my stay in hospital, my sister Wendy came up to Huddersfield to help me return to London so that I could fully recuperate from my operation. It was early November. I was going to miss the rest of the first term. It took a couple of days of serious thought, but I decided not to go back. There was nothing for me there any more. If it had been a course I cared about, then I would've found a way to make it work – but for Business Studies? Nah. Besides, it would take me until after Christmas before I was fit enough to travel and, quite frankly, my head was all over the place. I wasn't sure what I wanted any more, I just knew I didn't want to study maths and statistics, accounting, economics, marketing and most of the other topics on the course. Life was too short.

The time I had left was not going to be wasted.

As soon as I could, I headed to the local library to research my disorder. I knew that red blood cells were normally round and flexible, allowing them to move easily through blood vessels. I learned that with sickle cell anaemia, a proportion of red blood cells are shaped like sickles or quarter moons (hence the name) and this meant they carried less oxygen around the body, which could lead to extreme tiredness, swelling of the hands and feet, frequent infections and vision issues. Such cells also had the tendency to clump together, cutting off blood flow and oxygen to joints and organs, causing acute, excruciating pain. The more I read about the disorder, the more it explained. The days off school with unspecified pains in my stomach or joints; the weakness in my legs that I was teased about as a child – until I sought to do something about it by running around the block or the park and joining my school's rounders and tennis teams. I read about how stress, extreme tiredness, and being too cold or too hot could all trigger a sickle cell episode called a crisis.

While recuperating at home, I thought carefully about what I should do next. Now that I had my A-level results – I'd passed them all (in your face, Mrs T!) – I applied to Goldsmiths College to follow my original plan of studying for an English and Drama degree. My old sociology lecturer provided me with a reference and, after being invited in for an interview, I was accepted on the course, starting the following September.

Take a seat, Mrs T.

My future was finally back on track. Getting my A-level results and applying to Goldsmiths taught me a life lesson. I realised there were always going to be people who would try to slam doors in my face. There would always be those who tried to persuade me that this or that was not for the likes of me because of my class, gender or colour. That was their choice. How I handled their doubts, negativity, snobbery or outright racism was mine. I could either let them stop me in my tracks, I could waste my time and my life arguing with them, or I could find a way to go around them. The latter might make the route that much longer but so be it. Doing the latter would mean I never stopped or went backwards, but always kept moving. When Mrs T tried to justify her racism by stating that I wouldn't pass my English A-level anyway, I used that as a spur to work even harder just to prove her wrong. The choice to go to university immediately after school was taken out of my hands by Mrs T, who was ready to scupper my chances by writing me a bad reference. But all she did was slow me down, she didn't stop me. Applying to Goldsmiths directly meant I took my future out of Mrs T's hands and back into my own. Another life lesson learned. Onwards and upwards.

However, there was no getting around the fact that I had very little money. As I had officially given up my place at Huddersfield Poly, there was no prospect of any coming my way, either. My younger brothers were still at school and Mum and my older siblings didn't have money to spare. I was eighteen and rudderless.

It was time to get a job.

I visited the local job centre, but there were no jobs advertised that appealed or that I had the experience or qualifications for. By now I was down to my last five pounds. I decided to treat myself to a trip to the West End. What better way to pass some time than to lose myself among anonymous people.

It was a glorious crisp and clear winter's day. After the cost of a return train ticket and a burger, chips, and chocolate milk-shake for my lunch, I had exactly two pence left in my purse and no idea where the next penny was going to come from. I decided to cheer myself up by window shopping.

As I walked along Oxford Street, I ducked down Wardour Street on my way back to Charing Cross Station, rather than my usual route via Tottenham Court Road Station and then south along Charing Cross Road. I was tired and dispirited and every so often the thought would pop into my head that I wouldn't live long enough to draw a pension or have children or see in the twenty-first century or do something worthwhile with my life. Every so often, self-pity would wash over me and I would have to start jogging or even running to escape it. A sudden sprint, a sudden stop. Rinse and repeat. Lord knows what those around me thought I was doing. As I started to jog down Wardour Street, I saw a job centre on the right-hand side of the road. Well, I had nothing to lose, so I popped in. I scanned the index cards to see if anything vaguely suitable leapt out at me. There was a job for a documentation assistant at a software house just off Oxford Street. I took the card to one of the assistants and she phoned the company's HR department to give them my potted CV. They wanted to know my O- and A-level results, if I'd worked in the past and, if so, where and doing what? After giving out my details, there was silence on her side as she listened, then she put her hand over the mouthpiece and asked, 'Can you go for an interview now?'

'What? Right now?'

She nodded.

'But I'm not dressed for an interview,' I protested.

I was wearing black leggings and a brown-and-green patterned tabard over a brown T-shirt. My curly-perm afro wasn't even shaped, and I had on no make-up.

'You look fine. Shall I tell them you're on your way?' the job centre worker asked. 'They're less than five minutes away.'

I nodded. If they asked me to come for an interview the following day or week, I'd have to decline as I didn't have the cash to get me back to the West End, so why not? I had nothing to lose but time. I headed for the interview and after a thirty-minute chat I was offered the job on the spot and asked to start on Monday of the following week – 2 February.

There was no doubt what my answer would be. I'd have to borrow the train fare for the month off my aunt, promising to pay her back out of my first pay cheque, but *I had a job*. A full-time job. Yippee! I could work until September of that year, when my English and Drama degree was due to start, by which time I'd have savings in the bank – the perfect way to avoid the dire financial straits I'd encountered in Huddersfield.

It turned out 'documentation assistant' was a fancy title for a filing clerk. But I was working at a software house, full of computers. Plus, I was on a project with more than forty people, all of whom were white, and more than half of whom were men. The software house had Black employees, but they were all women and almost all typists, jammed together into a small space on the top floor. They sat at rows of desks, a golf-ball typewriter before each person. A true typing pool. It was a jarring image. Here was a bank of typists on the top floor, most of whom were Black. Why weren't they assigned to the various projects going on throughout the parts of the building used by the company? Why were they all stuck in one gloomy office on the top floor? Anyone from outside who was given a tour of the various projects would assume the employees there were entirely white. Or was that the point?

Maybe the person giving me the building tour saw the expression on my face because she rushed to explain, 'We have a central bank of typists who type up the reports from all the different departments as required. It would be too noisy to have typists working on every floor with each department. Their typewriters can be very loud.'

Hmm . . .

I was eighteen and wanted the job, so I wasn't about to argue. Besides, this was a means to an end, a way to make money, money, money until my degree began in September.

But I never started my English and Drama degree. Fate intervened.

Again.

As always.

25

The majority of the people on the project I was a part of were recent university graduates and only a few years older than me, which meant they were incredibly sociable. Even the managers, who were in their thirties and older, sometimes joined in our after-work activities. Lunchtimes were spent communally, eating kebabs or fish and chips around a big table, or heading off to a popular greasy spoon that served breakfast all day, as well as chips, peas and baked beans. At least two evenings a week were spent going to the pub to celebrate someone's birthday or just because. Most Wednesday lunchtimes, a number of us would go swimming at the pool on Marshall Street, which was only a ten-minute walk away. (I had a curly perm at the time so swimming wasn't the trial it had been at school.) One or two weekends a month were spent playing five-a-side football, squash or tennis at the affiliated sports club in Lower Sydenham. I was having the time of my life and enjoyed the company of most people on the project. Plus, it was the first time I'd encountered computers. I found them fascinating and wanted to learn a lot more about them. For a first full-time job, I felt I'd hit the jackpot.

On 13 April 1981, a Monday, I arrived at work and walked into the open plan to head for my desk – the same as I had done every morning since I'd started in February. A few metres from the door was a group of about ten or twelve colleagues – men and women – all talking in serious tones. Tones which fizzled, guttered and died the moment I appeared. Instinctively I knew what they'd been talking about – the Brixton riots that had happened at the weekend. Mum and I had spent the past forty-eight hours discussing them.

There was a gallows humour 'joke' in the Black community at the time stating that if a Black person walked into Stoke Newington Police Station, nine times out of ten they'd leave in an ambulance or a body bag. In February 1980, five units of the Special Patrol Group, a notorious paramilitary squad, began to operate in Hackney with no consultation or warning. When the leader of the council criticised the police for sanctioning this, Hackney's Police Commander Mitchell replied, 'I don't feel obliged to tell anyone about my policing activities.'

The police in Brixton were just as notorious. The overzealous implementation of stop-and-search became a tool for the intimidation of Black people. Many of us saw the riots as an act of standing up to the police after years of unchecked and vicious racist abuse.

But that was in the Black community. It was regularly reported in the Black press. In the white mainstream press? Not so much.

So here I was just entering the open-plan office, with a huddle of people already present and discussing the riots as I arrived – and then all conversation stopped. Head high, I gave them all my usual, 'Good morning,' and was making for my desk when one of them called me over. Heart thumping, I braced myself. Incoming! Shields up!

'Why . . . why do Black people riot?' said one of the managers, getting straight to the point.

'Why would you do that? Attack the police like that?' asked another.

I took a deep breath. Then another.

Keep your anger inside, Malorie. Be calm. Be fucking calm.

'First of all,' I began. *'I* didn't attack anyone. Nor did anyone else I know. And some, *some* Black people were rioting because the police in Brixton treat us Black people like less than dirt. Black men can't walk in Brixton or other parts of London without being thrown up against walls, stopped and searched and abused by racist police. You can only be pushed so far before you want to push back.'

'Yes, but white people don't do that,' said another.

'Because white people's experiences of dealing with the police is not the same as Black people's,' I said.

Murmurs.

Stares.

Glares.

All of my colleagues had heard me but most weren't listening. They didn't have the lived experience of being indiscriminately bullied and harassed simply because of the colour of their skin. They hadn't experienced it so, as far as they were concerned, it didn't or couldn't happen. I looked around the group confronting me, feeling like I and every other Black person in the country was on trial. Most of my work colleagues had never even spoken to a Black person before I joined the project, but they felt they knew everything about us.

'My aunt was mugged by a Black man,' said yet another. 'That's why I don't like Black people. I don't mean you, Lorie. You're all right, but not other Black people.'

'I'm Black,' I said, pointing out the obvious. 'If you don't like Black people that includes me. You're condemning me for the actions of some random arsehole mugger who just happened to be Black. If your aunt had been mugged or assaulted by a white person, would you be telling every other white person in this open plan that you don't like them because of it?'

'It's not the same,' she protested.

Yeah, it was obvious that to her mind it was completely different.

'If *you* people have a grievance then you should address it properly, not riot,' said the brunette woman who'd made a point of coming over on my first day to welcome me.

'Bollocks to this!' I thought.

'Hitler was responsible for the deaths of at least six million people and he was white,' I said. 'King Leopold of Belgium was responsible for the deaths of at least ten million Africans – he was white. Stalin – also white – was responsible for the deaths of twenty million. Pinochet has killed thousands – he's white. White people went to America and wiped out a number of Native American tribes. White people went to Tasmania and wiped out the Tasmanian aborigines. Why do you do that? Why do you have to be so aggressive?'

The protests came thick and fast.

'We're not all like that.'

'That's not the same thing and you know it.'

'How dare you?'

'What a stupid argument.'

I shook my head, perplexed as to why they could see it was an unfair and ridiculous argument one way but not the other. I was nineteen and being confronted by a number of white people all standing around me, bristling with hostility. For goodness' sake, I didn't believe for a moment that they were responsible for the actions of Pinochet and Hitler. In my experience, most people, whatever their background, just wanted to live and let live. My heart was drumming and I felt totally intimidated. Most of those around me were the same people I'd had lunch with and gone to the pub with on several occasions over the last few months. Now it felt like they were holding me personally responsible for the Brixton riots. I'm not going to lie, it felt like a lynch mob.

You didn't need to be a rocket scientist to figure it out, but it struck me that there were those in the group before me who didn't want to figure it out.

Tom Robinson's song '(Sing If You're) Glad to Be Gay', released a few years previously, chose that moment to start playing in my head. The song recounted the way the police treated gay people, which echoed the Black experience. It seemed to me that any minority was fair game for ill-treatment by the police, and the ones not affected would rather argue that it didn't happen than stand and face the ugly reality that it could and it did. Acknowledging what happened to some people in society at the hands of the police meant facing the fact it could happen to them. After all, if you couldn't trust the police – those tasked with protecting and helping us in times of trouble – then where did that leave any of us? As a consequence, some of my colleagues would rather believe that each and every stop-and-search was carried out for a legitimate reason, and not, all too often, based on skin colour.

I looked around at those before me, feeling their intense anger. I knew my counterargument was far too emotive to be effective, but it was all I had on the spur of the moment. They didn't want to hear the reasons why this was happening in Brixton. All they were focused on was the outcome of the rioting, not the cause. Black people rioting and breaking the law was evidence, in their eyes, that all Black people had a propensity for crime. This view, this false rationale, was everywhere in British society at the time. White criminals were a singular case. One white person committing a crime wasn't used as an example of an issue in the white community. And the more heinous their crime, the more the media and others would bend over backwards trying to explain or excuse away their actions as that of a 'lone wolf' or someone with 'mental challenges'. Black criminals weren't afforded the same understanding.

And an earnest disclaimer of, 'I don't like Black people but you're all right, Lorie,' was not the mitigation that person thought it was. I wasn't interested in being an exception for them.

If you're an immigrant or descended from migrants in this country, you're used and abused and forgotten. You're mistreated, bruised and battered. Picked on and put upon. If you point it out, you're playing the victim or 'race baiting'. You're constantly told to be a good immigrant and keep quiet about injustice. Don't complain, don't agitate, blend into the background, keep your mouth shut, be grateful you've even been allowed in the country – and we might let you stay. Maybe.

Without saying another word, I turned and headed back to my desk.

The temperature at work between me and a few of my colleagues was distinctly frosty for the next couple of days. There were the occasional whispers around me but I ignored them and got on with my work. And, in fairness, most people treated me exactly the same after the riots as they had treated me before them – with friendship, good humour and courtesy.

Some I worked with freely admitted that I was the first Black person with whom they'd ever had a prolonged conversation or shared a pint. The wilful ignorance of a few on the project was astounding, the false assumptions plentiful. The majority of people I was working with held university degrees. I thought that might denote some knowledge or sense of how others lived in our society, but I was wrong.

The next day, I was alone in the terminal room with Neil, a guy I'd met at work who had become a good friend. From the moment we were introduced, we got on like we'd known each other for years. He hadn't been present at the confrontation the day before so I told him what had happened, curious as to what his stance would be. I didn't have to wait long to find out. He was appalled that I'd been treated like that and he was furious that he hadn't been present to stand beside me. In fact he was ready to go confront his colleagues on my behalf. I practically had to hold him back. I just wanted to let the whole thing blow over.

Besides, after that day the riots weren't brought up again, at least not in front of me. The temperature in the open plan rose back up to normal levels. When Lord Scarman's report – which found evidence of the disproportionate use of stop-and-search against Black people – was published later that year, it received a comment or two and everyone moved on.

However, it was a life lesson learned.

26

On 18 February 1999, I sat down to watch the docudrama *The Murder of Stephen Lawrence*. I thought I knew the details of the case, having followed the story closely in the Black newspaper *The Voice* over the years since Stephen's murder. The names of his alleged assailants were common knowledge, but no one at that time had been charged with his murder. Nothing could've prepared me for what I watched that night.

On 22 April 1993, Stephen Lawrence, Black, eighteen, was waiting for a bus in Eltham, south-east London, with his friend Duwayne Brooks when they were jumped in an unprovoked attack by five white men and Stephen was stabbed several times. He tried to get away but collapsed and bled to death. Though several people came forward to name a local gang in connection with the crime, and Duwayne told the police what had happened, the Crown Prosecution Service decided to drop the case.

I watched the docudrama in astonishment. The initial police investigation had been so inadequate – and the way the Lawrence family were treated by the police was appalling. Suspicion even fell on Duwayne Brooks, albeit briefly. There was something about seeing the dramatisation that made me realise just how little I did know. Anger drilled into me deeper and deeper as I watched. And when I had finished watching, I felt . . . altered. Permanently changed.

And very, very angry.

In the days and weeks that followed, a few of the comments

I heard and read astounded me, so much so that I wondered if I'd watched the same programme.

'What were Stephen and his friend doing out so late?'

'Stephen and Duwayne must've done something to provoke the men who assaulted them. No one would just stab another person unprovoked like that.'

'Well, there had to be a reason for the police to act that way. Something about the Lawrence family that wasn't in the drama.'

I genuinely couldn't believe what I was hearing. The Macpherson Report (published in 1997) into Stephen Lawrence's murder and the subsequent police response concluded that the police investigation was 'marred by a combination of professional incompetence, institutional racism and a failure of leadership'. When I pointed this out to a friend, it was dismissed and glossed over with a, 'Well, the police aren't like that any more.'

I realised that some of my white colleagues just didn't get it because they'd never had to live through it. They'd never been stopped when travelling through customs at airports, they'd never been followed around shops and supermarkets by security staff convinced they were only there to steal something, they'd never had to prove that the car they were driving was theirs or been suspected of carrying drugs because of their skin colour, they'd never been told to go back to where they came from, spat at or elbowed into the street, they'd never been told that teaching or any other profession was not for them because of their melanin level. They'd never had to carry out extra research when determining whether to take a holiday or travel to new destinations (both foreign and domestic). They'd never had to scan new places and spaces for safety as a matter of survival.

I was convinced the absence of books, films and TV dramas featuring people of colour when my generation (and subsequent generations) was growing up played an important role in this lack of understanding. My white contemporaries hadn't learned as children to empathise with people outside their own colour, culture or heritage because they hadn't been shown lives other than their own. How can you read and watch what isn't available? And of the few such stories that did exist at the time, how many (before the 2000s) were straight-up adventures, mysteries, thrillers, fantasies or comedies – stories in which racism was not the major theme? I can't think of a single Hollywood or British film before the 2000s that featured a Black child as the main character. And even now I can count such films on the fingers of one hand.

Watching the drama about the Lawrences made me desperate to address all the thoughts buzzing like bees in my head – the assumptions and presumptions of the police, the victim-blaming, the negative way Stephen Lawrence was portrayed by some newspapers. I needed to do something about what I'd just seen. But what?

By 1999 I was firmly established as a writer. I had forty-nine books under my belt and I wanted to write something different for my fiftieth. I decided to write a story explicitly and overtly about racism. It was time to dust off an idea I'd had for quite some time, a story about a slave in the eighteenth century; a narrative that would move forward in time through our present and into the future. However, whenever I mentioned slavery as the topic of my next book to friends, the drawbridge would go up and the doubtful comments would come. The response was underwhelming to say the least.

'It's such a painful subject.'

'It was so long ago.'

'The subject matter is so depressing.'

Basically – 'Why go there?'

I realised that before I'd even written a single word, everyone

I spoke to assumed they already knew what the story would be about. I needed to come up with a story that would not just play with but confound people's expectations. However, it had to be absolutely grounded in the real world to be believable.

What if I were to write a story where white people were the ones treated like second-class citizens? What if they were the ones to suffer negative prejudgement in every societal setting based primarily on their skin colour? But how could I do this so that the conceit of the story wasn't immediately obvious? How about if I didn't describe my characters as white or Black but by other names – like Noughts and Crosses. Nought could be the collective name for white people, plus it sounded like zero or nothing, and that could denote how the Noughts in my world are considered, similar to how the word 'black' has a number of negative connotations in the English language. And Crosses could be Black people, who in my fictional world are considered closer to God in every way. That societal backdrop could be used to act as a potential block to my two main characters being permitted to live their lives together happily ever after. Hatred maims and kills – I didn't want to shy away from that.

That's how the story of *Noughts and Crosses* was born.

I toyed with other story titles – like 'Snakes and Ladders' as a metaphor for trying to get ahead, both personally and professionally – but decided to keep my original title. I reckoned it would work because noughts and crosses is the name of a game that no one plays past childhood as, once you know the rules, no one ever wins. It worked as a metaphor for racism – a way of thinking and being that ultimately diminishes us all. So what's the point of it? Bigotry and prejudice are never just black-and-white, binary issues; there are nuances of behaviour, perception, culture, expectation, religion and a host of other factors that come into play. I wanted my story to be not just about skin colour but perceived class as well. I decided that if I told the story from the point of view of a naive thirteen-year-old – Persephone – *and* not-so-naive fifteen-year-old – Callum – then I could explore and confront the realities of their world as they grow older and more aware.

First and foremost, however, I wanted the story to be about Callum and Sephy and their friendship, which develops into something stronger and deeper. Any plot points that didn't serve their story would have to be ruthlessly omitted. And writing from both their points of view would force me to be even-handed in the telling of their stories. I wasn't telling *my* story, I was telling theirs, and I needed to make sure that my own views didn't creep into my characters' mouths or actions. As I've already mentioned, writing this novel was different to the ones that had gone before because Callum and I shared certain experiences – which meant I could write them from memories rather than having to create them from scratch.

Anger planted me in my chair in front of my computer every day for the year it took me to write *Noughts and Crosses*. Living with Callum and Sephy in my head for that length of time was immensely enjoyable and unexpectedly painful. Enjoyable because the story was meshing together as I had planned. Painful because writing Callum's life, especially when he was at school, dragged up some personal, scratchy memories of my own.

Anger also drove me to write my novel *Boys Don't Cry*, after reading about a brutal homophobic attack on a 62-year-old gay man in London's Trafalgar Square – the man died of his injuries eighteen days later. The novel is about two brothers, Dante and Adam. Dante's ex-girlfriend dumps their baby on him, telling him she can't cope and she's not coming back. Adam is gay and a toxic relationship leads to him reassessing exactly what he wants from his life.

Not long after this book was first published, I was invited to speak at an event in Brixton. As I spoke about the inspiration for *Boys Don't Cry* and its plot and themes, a Black man in his mid-forties in the audience started tutting and kissing his teeth loudly and shifting like his chair had suddenly caught fire and he was strapped to it. This man glared at me like I was his worst enemy – and I knew why. He was unhappy that one of my main characters, Adam, was Black, gay, out and proud. Every time I mentioned Adam, the tutting and disapproving noises grew louder. Ignoring him, I continued with my presentation. When I had finished, the man made a point of standing up, turning round and walking out. As far as I was concerned, his anger only confirmed that I'd been right to write the book in the first place.

It wasn't the first time I'd been confronted by an angry adult displeased at the subject matter I'd chosen for one of my books. A white man once berated me for writing *Pig-Heart Boy*.

'No child wants to read about their own mortality. That's not a children's book, it's a book for adults,' he told me, his expression thunderous.

'There are children who are chronically ill and there are children who are dying,' I replied carefully. 'Are you saying that they should be hidden away or that they shouldn't see themselves in the books they might read?'

'No child wants to read about that,' the man insisted.

What he meant of course was that he didn't want to read about that – which was fair enough – and he wanted to impose his view on my readership – which was not fair enough.

'I hope my book will provide information and strategies for discussion should a child find themselves in a comparable situation or know someone who is going through something similar,' I told him. 'Children aren't invincible or invulnerable. Don't you think they deserve stories that acknowledge that?'

'Well, if it were up to me, I'd withdraw that book from publication,' he told me before walking off.

'Lucky it isn't up to you then,' I thought.

A number of my books have drawn criticism, sometimes angry criticism from adults regarding the subject matter. Their anger feeds me. It lets me know that I must be doing something right. There have been times when I've sat down to write a new book and one of my first thoughts has been, 'I'm going to get a right kicking for this one!' but that has never, *ever* stopped me from writing my story.

As I stated previously, for a long time, I tried not to embrace or embody the tedious angry Black woman stereotype. But here's the thing: wrath has benefits! It sharpens the focus, energises us and, fundamentally, promotes survival. It also motivates us to solve problems. Anger makes me stand up and speak up. It also makes me sit down and write. If stories like *Noughts and Crosses*, *Pig-Heart Boy* or *Boys Don't Cry* make some adults uncomfortable, then so be it. Will that ever stop me? Hell no!

Like I said, anger gets shit done.

27

No matter how stoic or patient, you can only be pushed so far before you want, need or long to push back. Hard. When you're the focus of constant hatred, eventually you want to repay like for like. It's so easy for hate to breed more hate, and it takes real strength of character to rise above it. Strength I struggled to find as a teenager. I was bewildered. Defensive. Angry. Hate was spreading through me like a vicious cancer. Fed up with being a victim, I vowed never to be one again. But closing yourself from being hurt means closing yourself off entirely. That's what I did for a couple of years. And closing myself off entirely meant losing myself. I was a tree with no roots. I didn't belong anywhere. I had a stake in nothing. I was a nowhere child.

When it comes to writing books, I always work longest and hardest on creating my characters. It doesn't matter if a book tells the wildest fantasy, the strangest horror, the weirdest flight of fancy – if the reader doesn't believe in or cannot relate to the protagonist and their dilemmas then the whole story falls apart.

I remember sending my mum a proof of *Noughts and Crosses* once it became available and before it hit the shops. She phoned me a day later in a right mood having read fifty-something pages and had questions!

'Is Callum Black or white?' she asked, getting right to the point.

'He's white, Mum,' I replied.

'Meggie's son is white?'

'Yes, Mum.'

'Hang on. So is Sephy Black or white?'

'She's Black, Mum.'

Mum kissed her teeth. 'I thought it was the other way around. Now I'm going to have to reread the book from the beginning again,' she said, putting down the phone.

I laughed, knowing in that moment that I'd achieved what I set out to do. I wanted to write a story which played with the reader's assumptions. In fact, I only mentioned skin colour once in the entire book. The characters were Noughts and Crosses or, known by their derogatory names, 'blankers' and 'daggers'.

I knew the subject matter was bound to make some adults uncomfortable, and uncomfortable people tend not to appreciate those who make them feel that way. As the late, great writer Maya Angelou once said, 'I've learned that people will forget what you said, people will forget what you did, but people will never forget how you made them feel.' I had no doubt that teens would embrace the themes in the book and, if I did my job properly, would believe in Callum and Sephy, their lives, their choices, their dilemmas. I also didn't doubt that some adults would decry my story as not being suitable for young adults, as a story that should never have been told, as a fake fictional story because 'Britain isn't like that', as too racy, too sexy, too much love, too much hate, just too much. But that wasn't going to stop me from writing the story my way. Besides, I knew I wouldn't be able to write another story until I got *Noughts and Crosses* out of my system.

The book was finally published. It ticked along for a bit and got some reasonable reviews as well as some unfavourable reviews. One I particularly remember stated, 'I would've been more impressed if this story of racism was written by a white author. That would've shown some real insight.' I realised in that moment that, for some critics, any work produced by a

Black artist was not and never would be enough. It saddens me that some view any creative endeavour that features people of colour as a zero-sum game: for someone to win, someone else has to lose. If there are more books published, more film and TV programmes made, more theatre productions staged that feature Black protagonists, then that must mean there will be fewer with white protagonists. Those people long for their world to be exclusively white. If a library contains 1,000 books, all of which feature white protagonists, and one is replaced by a book that features a Black protagonist, they will only see the one book which they deem to have taken a white person's space and place – never the 999 books featuring white main characters still left on the shelves.

I remember watching Toni Morrison being interviewed by the Australian journalist Jana Wendt, who asked her when she was going to write white lives into her books in a substantial way. Toni Morrison pointed out in her steady, considered manner, 'You can't understand how powerfully racist that question is, can you? 'Cause you could never ask a white author, "When are you going to write about Black people?" – whether he did or not or she did or not. Even the enquiry comes from a position of being in the centre.'

A point Wendt acknowledged by saying, 'And being used to being in the centre.'

In all fairness, Wendt seemed to take the comment on board, but it was fascinating to me that she felt it was even a question.

Before *Noughts and Crosses* was published, I myself had been asked, at more than one literary or school event, why I only write about Black people.

Though the mindset that white people must be centred in every story is finally changing, there is still work to do on this front, especially as there are, at the time of writing, political manoeuvres taking place in some school districts in America to ban young adult books that address race or racism. This is also happening with YA books that feature LGBTQ+ protagonists. Books featuring main characters from all backgrounds help to banish ignorance and promote understanding. Maybe that's what some school boards or officials are afraid of?

The beauty of writing for children and young adults is that your readers' minds are still open, and they have a greater willingness to hop on board any story that entertains and engages, or that may challenge their thinking. I once had an adult reader of *Noughts and Crosses* berate me at a literary festival for my story setting, stating, 'Your story isn't true. Black people aren't the ones in power or in the majority in Britain. That's not the way it is.'

Well, duh!

That's why my book is classed as *fiction*.

Young adults just get it. They understand what I am trying to do in a way that some adults can't or simply refuse to.

Some adults really do my head in!

28

Something I didn't expect when my sickle cell was first diagnosed was the scepticism – the doubt – I received from some medical professionals. Let me call it what it is – the racism. How can a disorder I was born with invoke racism? These are some of the comments I've had said to me by medical staff over the years:

'I'm sure it can't hurt as much as you people make out.'

'You people are too keen to take drugs.'

'SHUT UP.' A white nurse screamed that at me once in Lewisham Hospital when I was crying with pain. 'SHUT UP.'

She returned after an hour to apologise, but 'SHUT UP' still rings in my head.

Once, when I was in hospital going through yet another excruciating sickle cell crisis, I kept ringing the buzzer for my overdue pain relief and I kept being ignored. Every time a nurse passed my bed I asked for my meds – and was ignored. I asked two doctors who passed my bed for pain relief and was told to ask one of the nurses. I felt like I was being sawn in half, the pain was that intense, but I was still being deliberately ignored. After an hour of this, and at the end of my tether, I SCREAMED! Loud and long. Long and loud. The sound filled the ward. The sister came running over to my bed.

'Please don't do that,' she scowled.

'Why are you ignoring me?' I asked, bewildered. 'I'm in a great deal of pain. And I was due my pain relief over an hour ago.'

The nurse looked me in the eye and said in all seriousness, 'I do have patients, you know.'

'Aren't I a patient too?' I asked.

She started at my words, like she hadn't even considered that before. Like I'd given her food for thought. Another twenty minutes later (as a lesson for screaming, I suppose), I finally received my pain relief.

Over the years, I've listened to senior doctors berating junior doctors for not taking sickle cell seriously. For not taking me and my pain seriously. Once, I explained to a new doctor who wanted to take my medical history that the full name for what I had was 'sickle cell beta thalassemia'.

'There's no such thing,' he scoffed.

He was the second doctor to say that to me since I'd been diagnosed in 1980. I had to force myself to breathe in, breathe out, not scream, not shout. I sat perfectly still as I looked at the doctor and thought, 'Check this guy. If he hasn't heard of it, then it doesn't exist, or I made it up or got it wrong.' I'm sad to say that his statement and his reaction was and is par for the course when it comes to sickle cell care and treatment, at least in my forty-plus years of experience.

After my last disastrous stay in Lewisham Hospital back in 1998, I promised myself I would never enter another hospital again unless Death was not just beckoning me through his door but had grabbed me by my hand to drag me after him. No more hospitals until then.

But sometimes the sickle cell pain hits and grips, slices and dices and explodes like a bomb inside me. Not just once but over and over. It doesn't let go and my painkillers don't even touch the sides. Sometimes a sickle cell episode, or crisis, as they are called, makes a liar out of me and then I have no choice but to visit my local hospital.

The last hospital trip was in 2021. I literally couldn't move. I couldn't even get out of the bed for my hubby to drive me to hospital. Neil had no choice but to phone for an ambulance. The paramedic asked me if I wanted to go to King's College Hospital (where they know the difference between sickle cell and a hole in the ground) or my local hospital, the Princess Royal. I foolishly chose the latter. Big mistake. I was admitted on a Friday night. The pain relief I was offered for the entire weekend? Paracetamol.

'I have paracetamol at home,' I protested. 'Why would I come to hospital for paracetamol?'

'That's all you've been written up for,' I was told.

I was given one bag of saline intravenously. I should've been hydrated for a minimum of forty-eight hours. I tried to tell them, but no one would listen. The oxygen mask was taken off my face after half an hour, even though I was still struggling to breathe. It was a dark night, raining continuously from the time I was admitted. For the whole miserable weekend there was no sunshine, just charcoal-grey clouds, pouring rain and paracetamol. If I could've walked more than a step or two, I would've asked Neil to take me home.

Monday morning arrived bringing doctors to my bed who were full of apologies and pens to prescribe proper medication. Note to self, written several times in the past – but there's always room to underline them: *Don't get ill at the weekend.*

A doctor usually based at King's College Hospital came to see me. He apologised again and assured me that next time I would get better treatment, as I was now on the hospital database with a proper care plan in place.

It's been more than forty years since my disorder was diagnosed, and I *still* have to fight for proper care, for the appropriate pain relief, proper hydration methods, adequate oxygen when required. I still struggle to find medical staff who have a clue.

And God, I'm so tired of it all. Exhausted.

Sickle cell makes me miserable.

Sickle cell makes me rude.

I admit it.

My patience is minimal, and my manners fly out the window when I'm being cut to pieces with cheese wire, or my joints are being squeezed in a vice that grows tighter with every beat of my heart, and I'm only offered paracetamol for the pain.

For too long I was angry at and resentful of my diagnosis and all the things I thought it had taken away from me. My existence has spiralled around sickle cell all my life, even when I didn't know what I had. There were bouts of weakness and several bouts of illness that went unexplained when I was a child and teenager, which were simply put down to me being a sickly child.

I suffered from two or three crises a year in my thirties and forties, but when I hit my mid-fifties, my health declined sharply. I had three years in my mid-fifties when I missed so much, including literary festival events at Hay, Edinburgh and Bath, because of sickle cell. I was having two or three crises a month. There was a time when I was afraid to travel in case I had a crisis. Being far away from home and having a crisis is no joke.

I had to think long and hard about taking on the role of Children's Laureate in 2013. I wanted to do the job properly, to do it justice. Could I do so if I was ill all the time? I decided that with careful management, and a lot of luck, I'd be OK. So I said yes to the role and during my two-year tenure only missed one event, in Edinburgh, because of a crisis.

It was absolutely no one's fault, just one of those things. And I'm sure that if I'd made it known that I had sickle cell, and had to be careful not to get too tired, then allowances would have been made. But the thing is, I never told colleagues – or even certain friends – about my sickle cell. I kept it quiet because when you have an ailment, a disorder or a disease, that's all people can talk about. You stop being a person and become your condition.

'How are you feeling?'

'How are you coping?'

'How is your work with sickle cell?'

'How is your world with sickle cell?'

'How is your life with sickle cell?'

Bollocks to sickle cell! I am more than an ailment, a disorder, a genetic dysfunction. And I consider myself lucky that it doesn't make its presence felt all the time. Although this is both a blessing and a curse. When I'm not suffering from a crisis, I function the same as everyone else. But when a crisis hits, it comes at you with the force of a wrecking ball. And crises can hit without warning so that you're fine one minute and in agony the next. No doubt this has led to accusations made to some sickle cell sufferers of 'putting it on' or exaggerating their symptoms.

Recently, there has been talk of disorders such as sickle cell and cystic fibrosis being screened for before birth, with the suggestion they may ultimately be eradicated. In a parallel world where such screening already takes place, was I even born? Or was I born with the sickle cell gene removed or switched off in the womb? I do sometimes wonder, because my disorder led directly to my career as an author. I mean, *directly*. It gives me pause to consider whether, in a perfect world, I would even exist.

In that parallel world of gene perfection, did my disorder make me less than? Not worth saving? Was it suggested to my parents that they have an abortion to spare me and them the pain of my existence, the bouts of weakness, the trips to hospital, the state expense of my care? I hasten to add that I'm no anti-abortionist. I believe every woman has the right to choose what is best for them and their circumstances. That choice should not lie in the hands of the state or men who have decided they are entitled to make decisions on women's behalf.

But sickle cell has shaped my life and made me who I am. The band Imagine Dragons sing my life in their song 'Believer' – it might've been written for me! So here's what I do. I live for the moments in-between. The moments when I wake up to a new day and I'm pain-free. And on such days, I smile a little too much and laugh a little too loudly and speak a little too unguard-edly and live a little too exuberantly because the in-between moments are the best. And it's curious that I should call such times the in-between moments because luckily they are in the majority. But the crisis moments rip deeper into my flesh and hold on harder and sometimes feel like I'll never shake them off.

I try to make my life about the in-between moments. I wake up and thank God for each new morning; every new day is more than I was promised, a lot more than I overheard that I would get. And I'm grateful.

If I could, would I wish that I never had sickle cell?

Hell no! It made me an author, a fighter, a survivor.

I can live with that.

29

I'm a huge fan of the brilliant Steven Spielberg film *Minority Report* starring Tom Cruise and Samantha Morton. It is set in 2054, when three clairvoyants – 'precogs' – visualise impending homicides, with projections of their visualisations used to determine where the imminent crime will occur. This lets the police arrest the perpetrator *before* the crime happens. And no one has a problem with this system until the precogs predict that Captain John Anderton, the lead officer of the programme (played by Tom Cruise), will murder someone he doesn't know in less than thirty-six hours. Profiling at its most extreme!

Racial profiling is the act of being suspected, targeted or discriminated against on the basis of your ethnicity rather than on available evidence or actual individual suspicion. It's hard to convey to those who don't experience it just how pervasive and damaging profiling, particularly racial profiling, can be. You are effectively deemed guilty before the fact.

If I go shopping and buy anything with a security tag on it, I always ask the cashier to double check that it has been removed. And even then, I clutch my receipt in my hand rather than bury it in my handbag or pockets to prove to shop security that I paid for my purchases should the shop alarm go off – which has happened, and more than once.

Neil deGrasse Tyson, the renowned astrophysicist, has talked about his own experience of racial profiling. During a 2009 panel discussion hosted by the Center for Inquiry, he said:

I have security following me every time I go through department stores, presuming I'm a thief. I walked out of a store one time and the alarm went off and so they came running to me. I walked through the gate at the same time as a white male walked through the gate. And that guy just walked off with the stolen goods, knowing they would stop me and not him.

I find flying anywhere fraught as I'm so often pulled over by customs, who demand to search my luggage. I once tried to exit via the green channel and was stopped by a customs officer who wanted to check my suitcase. He was opening it when my husband came up behind me, as he'd had to wait a little longer for his own suitcase to hit the baggage carousel. The moment Neil appeared at my side and asked what was going on, the customs officer asked, 'Are you two together?'

'Yes,' Neil frowned. 'I'm her husband. Is there a problem?'

The customs officer immediately zipped up my suitcase and handed it back to me, then waved us through the green channel. I was *livid*. But, not wishing to subject myself to a vindictive cavity search, I had to hold my tongue. We got through the green channel and then I let rip at my poor hubby, because the whole sorry incident had been some bullshit. A Black woman travelling on her own? Well, she must be a drugs mule. A Black woman travelling with her white husband? Oh, that's all right then. Wave her through.

There's a scene in *Noughts and Crosses* where Callum and Sephy are on a train and the ticket inspector is giving Callum a hard time for travelling in first class. After all, how could someone like him possibly afford a first-class ticket? This actually happened to me when I was nineteen or twenty, so writing that scene didn't require any stretch of the imagination. And the deference the ticket inspector pays to Sephy and Callum when Sephy intervenes was based on remembrances, rather than flights of fancy.

Driving is fraught. I drive a hybrid SUV and every time I pass a police car or see one behind me I fully expect to be pulled over and asked to prove that I own the car I'm driving.

Hospital care is fraught.

The justice system is fraught.

The education system is fraught.

The workplace is fraught.

Creative spaces are fraught. A friend told me about a white actor friend of hers who complained when they had lost out on an acting job to a Black actor because the producer/director must have had a quota to fill or an agenda to observe. Insulting, much? If this actor had lost out to another white actor, they would've sucked it up and accepted they weren't right for the role. But to lose to an actor of colour? The only explanation must be that there was an ulterior 'political correctness' motive. It can't be that the other actor was just . . . wait for it . . . better. No, it must be down to some form of affirmative action. Give me a break!

Are you Black with a job in the public eye?

You only got the job because someone somewhere had a quota to fill.

I remember when I was first announced as Children's Laureate and was doing the initial round of media interviews. One journalist asked me pointedly, 'What makes you qualified to take on such a high-profile role?'

I checked with some of the other Children's Laureates if they'd ever been asked such a question. None of them had.

And on and on it goes.

And when it stops, nobody knows.

Damn, but just living is fraught.

We Black people are not permitted to simply be good enough.

In the UK, if a Black person achieves something, the narrative runs that they must've been given it by white people. It's so tiring. Almost every Black person on Twitter I know personally has changed their Twitter handle to 'X is tired' at some point. Dealing with racism or potential racism day in, day out is exhausting – mentally and physically.

Recently I heard a saying: 'When the colour of your skin is seen as a weapon, you will never be seen as unarmed.'

And it's so true. You will always be treated as dangerous. As different. As a threat.

But I hold on to the hope that things will get better, even if they have to get worse first. Maybe I'm too much of a *Star Trek* fan and believe in a future where racism, sexism, homophobia and transphobia are merely historical terms. Maybe I'm a fool for holding on to the hope that the human race will get its act together in terms of how we treat each other and the planet before it's too late. Maybe . . .

30

I've learned over the years to be very careful in all my dealings with the press. Media outlets are businesses and make their money via advertising. And advertisers don't cough up if there's no one to advertise to. That's why the mainstream media love clickbait headlines and controversy. Controversy and misery sell papers – online and printed.

Online news has led to the advent of the clickbait heading.

Subeditors write provocative, salacious or incorrect headings to get people to click on their stories. And then they move on to the next article, not waiting around to see the consequences of their actions.

In August of 2014, during my tenure as Children's Laureate, I was interviewed by Richard Suchet of Sky News at the Edinburgh International Book Fair. I was asked about diversity in children's books (being a Black author, I get asked that question a lot! Actually, I don't mean a lot, I mean *always*). Now, whenever I get asked that question, I frame my answer from the heart but very carefully, knowing that there are some who are ready to peck me to pieces for the slightest infraction – as they see it.

So I spoke about how much work had been done in the area, but how there was definitely more to do. (Still true.) There was and is room for more writers and illustrators creating books that feature children and young adults from Traveller or Romany backgrounds, children with mental and physical challenges, children of colour and LGBTQ+ teens, plus children of different classes, cultures and religions. I talked about how creators from diverse backgrounds should be able to tell whatever stories they want, where their protagonist may or may not reflect their own heritage, circumstances or upbringing and how not every book a child or young adult reads needs to be an 'issues' book. It really does make a difference for all our children to be able to see themselves reflected in the books they read. Every child deserves to read different stories reflecting the world we live in – and beyond. They need to know they are not alone. Reading about characters with different backgrounds and concerns to our own also makes a difference in terms of empathy and understanding, and God knows we need more of that on this planet.

That's the gist of what I said.

Sky News broadcast the interview on air, and they also wrote it up for their online news channels with the headline 'Children's Laureate says there are "too many white faces in children's literature".' They had the 'too many white faces' in quotes. How do you put something that I never said in quotes?

And. Oh. My. God!

The story went out and my social media timelines lit up like an explosion at a fireworks factory. I was flooded with abuse, vitriol and pure, naked, ugly racism.

'This isn't your fucking country. Go back to where you came from, you monkey.'

'Fuck you. This is a white country. You don't belong.'

'How dare you? Most children in this country are white. No one wants to read about your kind. Go back to the banana republic you were born in.' (I was born in Clapham.)

And those were the milder messages.

On and on it went. Hundreds and hundreds of tweets and Facebook posts filled to overflowing with toxic hatred. I'd happened to go on Twitter before even seeing the Sky News headline, so to say I was blindsided would be a gross under-statement. I read through disgusting tweet after disgusting tweet wondering where on earth they had all come from. What had happened to spark all this hatred? Each message was a gut punch. After reading a number of these tweets, I scrolled back and started reporting them one by one. Big mistake. All that did was remove them from my Twitter timeline. I should've taken screenshots, composed a file and reported each and every low-life to the police. But I thought Twitter would do more than just remove the tweets from my timeline. I said then and I say again now – not once did the phrase in the banner headline pass my lips, because I don't think in those terms. I went on Face-book and Twitter to defend myself but it felt like whistling in a hurricane.

On the same day I tried to defend myself online, James Mat-thews, the Scotland bureau chief at Sky News, tweeted, 'Our headline writers are changing that headline and pass on their apologies.' Now, it wasn't Richard Suchet's fault; he apparently had nothing to do with the headline that was given to the art-icle. But by now I was receiving death threats and threats of physical harm – not just against me but against my husband and especially my daughter. Threats of rape and violence and worse.

Oh, hell no!

The stunned, rabbit-in-headlines shock I felt when I read through the first hundred or so messages now morphed into something far more fiery. Stating that I was furious doesn't even begin to touch the sides of what I was feeling. Big mistake on the part of those who threatened my family.

I tweeted, 'Hell will freeze over before I let racists and haters silence me. In fact, they just proved to me that I was right to speak out.'

Sky News changed the headline on the article, but by then it was too late. The damage had been done. The comments beneath their online article were horrifying in their racism and a friend sent me a photo of a news report from an Indian newspaper which had used the exact same headline.

As the saying goes, a lie can travel around the world in the time it takes the truth to pull on its boots. The only bright spot in the whole debacle was the number of authors, illustrators and others who contacted me directly and via social media to let me know they were standing with me. They rushed to my defence and took on those posting poison. That's the part – the only part – that brought tears to my eyes. I genuinely did feel like there were others who had my back, front and both sides. It was comforting to know, because it took another month, at least, for the vitriol to stop and for the haters to move on to their next target.

I now keep the following in mind whenever I have to deal with the mainstream media: there is no such thing as 'off the record' – even if you ask them to not report on something. The simple lesson is: if you don't want it aired, don't say it. Choose your words very carefully. There are those who delight in twisting every word and shining the worst possible light on anything you say. If you're being interviewed, the interviewer will most likely want to record it for their notes / write up afterwards. Make sure you record the interview as well for your own files and peace of mind. If you are misreported, get on top of that right away. Get the news outlet to change it and make sure you broadcast any and everywhere you can that you have been misquoted. If and when threatened by people on social media, don't rely on social media companies to clean house, do it yourself. Take screenshots, screenshot details of the sender of the threat, get as much info as you can from their metadata and then take copies of everything before handing over your file to the police. That's what I should've done and to this day I regret not doing so.

And, most important of all, don't take that shit lying down.

31

The Conservative government, in office and power since 2010, has managed to do something that extreme right-wing groups in Britain, including the National Front, the BNP and the EDL, had never managed before. They made me question my place in Britain. They made me wonder if I was even truly British, even though I was born here and my mum has a British passport. They brought in laws stating that being born here isn't enough to ensure your place on British soil.

There have been cases of people born here being deported to countries they had never seen or had only visited on the occasional holiday. There have been more cases of people who came to Britain as children and who, after living here for several decades, are now being told that they don't belong and will be deported. They've grown up in this country, had jobs, paid taxes, had families – but apparently that's not enough.

If my mum and sister had slacked on getting their naturalisation papers, they too would've been unceremoniously booted out. Never mind that my sister Wendy came over to the UK when she was very young. Never mind that my mum has been in this country for over sixty years. None of that matters. They would've been booted out.

In 2010, the Home Office destroyed the disembarkation cards and documentation of thousands of Caribbean children joining their parents, only to demand years later that they produce the self-same documentation to prove they had a right to stay in Britain. Vans were driven around London telling us to 'Go

Home'. Don't tell me that the messages on the vans were aimed at illegal immigrants, because it sure as hell didn't feel that way. The government stated that they wanted to create a 'hostile environment'. They succeeded: slow clap. The Brexit vote was a victory for the racists who felt there were too many immigrants in Britain and that voting for Brexit would rectify that. Now that's not to say that everyone who voted for Brexit was a racist; I don't believe that. But I do believe that the vast majority of racists in the UK voted for Brexit. There is a difference. The day after the Brexit referendum confirmed that Britain would indeed withdraw from Europe, I expressed my disappointment on Twitter. A woman tweeted back stating, 'Well you would say that because you're not really British,' to which I replied, 'And thus it begins.'

And thus it did.

I remember shopping in Marks and Sparks that same week and having another white woman barge me out of the way to get the tin she wanted, despite the fact that's what I was reaching for. She gave me a look, daring me to challenge her behaviour. After all, this was her country, not mine. I looked at her, saying nothing, waiting for her to speak. It had been a long time since I'd felt the irrepressible desire to rip out some woman's hair at the roots, but I was getting there. Maybe she saw how angry I was growing because she quickly moved on. I stood still until I had simmered down, 'cause the mood I was in, if anyone had looked at me sideways, I would've taken their head off. Over the coming weeks, I was convinced I must've time-travelled in my sleep and woken up in the 1970s. I had more verbal racist abuse directed at me in the weeks following the Brexit vote than I'd experienced in the three decades preceding it. It genuinely felt like I needed to be prepared to defend myself against verbal and even physical attacks at any time. The racists had crawled out from beneath their toadstools and too many people of colour were getting it – both barrels – on social media and in person.

In 2019, I watched a BBC documentary – *The Unwanted*, presented by David Olusoga – about the number of Black people of the Windrush generation who had been interned like they were criminals for not having the 'proper papers'. Having a National Insurance number was not enough. Working and paying taxes for over forty years in a number of cases was not enough. It was as if the government had decided that these Black people, many of whom were now of retirement age, were no longer useful. And therefore it was not just right but proper to kick them out of the UK with a leaflet telling them how to survive in their destination country, which some hadn't seen since childhood and others had never visited at all. Too many were denied healthcare, welfare benefits and the right to work, leaving them effectively destitute.

It was against this political backdrop that I was offered a CBE.

The Tory government have invested serious time and money to tell me and mine that we don't belong, that sixty years or more in this country aren't enough to call it home. They've effectively told us that we're not wanted, and then I'm offered a CBE? For what? For being lucky enough not to get my arse interned or deported?

I drafted my response, as follows:

The current political climate reinforces the notion that me and mine are neither welcome nor wanted in this country. The Windrush debacle in particular, rhetoric regarding immigrants, vehicles declaring that people like me should 'go home', etc. have all reinforced the fact that the country in which I was born and always considered my home and my own, sadly does not regard me in the same way. Therefore how can I in good faith and in good conscience accept a CBE? I thank you however for your consideration.

After adding my response to the bottom of the CBE form, I returned it.

Now, I'm not in any way disparaging or maligning any other person of colour who has accepted a state honour. All power to their elbow. It's a decision each and every person offered such an award has to make for themselves. I myself accepted an OBE for services to children's literature back in 2008, which, after much soul searching, I indeed felt honoured to receive. I'm not going to lie, I was flattered to be given the acknowledgement; plus, my mum threatened to kick my butt if I didn't take it! Although leaving the EU was already being touted as an objective by UKIP and others on the far right in 2008, my friends, colleagues and I never considered that such an extreme, right-wing, bat-shit idea would ever come into being. Why would Britain leave the EU when the benefits of membership were so obvious?

There were of course other considerations regarding accepting the OBE. I might wish that they would change the word 'empire' to 'excellence' or some such, but that's another discussion. And back then I felt like I was British whatever the racists might say.

But to accept a CBE awarded under 2019's Tory government just didn't sit well with me. Not when I'm still burning at the way in which too many people of the Windrush era are being treated. Not when, at the time of writing, the majority of those wrongly interned or deported are still waiting to be paid compensation.

So thanks for your consideration, but no thanks.

Perseverance

32

Nana korobi, ya oki – a Japanese phrase that means 'Fall down seven times, get up eight'. Every culture has a similar saying, whether it's, 'If at first you don't succeed, try, try again,' or the chorus of Chumbawamba's song 'Tubthumping'! Achievement doesn't just stem from having the natural aptitude or wherewithal to follow a dream, it's also about having the perseverance to do so. The journey from who we are to who we want to be can be long, possibly circuitous, and occasionally arduous, but my philosophy has always been 'eyes on the prize'. However, it took me a while to figure out just what prize I wanted to pursue.

In the mid-1980s I was in my early twenties. I had a well-paid job as project manager in an IT organisation, I had obtained an HNC (Higher National Certificate) in Computing from Thames Polytechnic by attending evening classes, and had finished my HND (Higher National Diploma) year but had not sat the exam. My job involved trips abroad, I had a company car, private health insurance and had played the spots off my *Purple Rain* and *Songs From The Big Chair* CDs – but I was growing increasingly unhappy. Though I'd long ago ceased to be angry about my limited lifespan, it felt like my life was an hourglass and the sand remaining was moving more and more rapidly in only one direction. I had six or seven years left. Did I really want to spend them in the world of computing? The prospect grew less and less appealing with each passing day. But what could I do instead? I had no idea. All I knew was I wanted to do something more creative, more fulfilling. A life of work, home and an occasional holiday wasn't enough.

One evening, while walking back to Charing Cross train station from a pancake eatery in Holborn, I was heading south along Drury Lane when I saw a sign on a lamp post for the City Literary Institute in Stukeley Street where acting, dancing and musical instrument lessons were available. I'd never heard of the place but as I was less than a minute away, I decided to check it out. It turned out they offered far more than was advertised on the lamp-post billboard. They ran all kinds of acting classes for every level (from an introduction to acting to method acting to comedy skills), creative writing classes that catered for complete beginners right up to workshops for professionals, history, languages, arts and crafts — and that was just the tip of the iceberg. Their prospectus was huge. The City Lit was a creative oasis and just what I was looking for.

After reading carefully through the prospectus, I made my choice – saxophone lessons. I'd always wanted to learn how to play the saxophone. Songs like Bill Withers's 'Just the Two of Us', featuring Grover Washington Jr on sax, Gerry Rafferty's 'Baker Street', featuring Raphael Ravenscroft, and Dave Brubeck's 'Take Five', featuring Paul Desmond, had long cemented my love of the instrument. But first I had to buy one. And – damn, but they were expensive! I justified the cost of one by telling myself that I would never stop having sax lessons and I would take practising seriously. Two weeks and one gorgeous Yamaha alto saxophone later, I signed up for lessons. The very first song we learned was Herbie Hancock's 'Watermelon Man' – the first few bars only, of course! And that was the first – but by no means the last – course that I took at the City Lit.

The sax classes did the trick for a while, but they weren't

enough. One evening I was having coffee during a lesson break, when I overheard some drama students talking about how much they were enjoying their course.

Acting?

Acting!

I'd always wanted to learn how to act. Giving up my place on the Goldsmiths College English and Drama degree to stay in computing had thwarted that. But hadn't I spent years practising being many different people in many different scenarios as I walked to and from school? Hadn't I always played out imaginary conversations in my head before writing them down in the stories I still occasionally worked on? So why not give lessons a go? Then I could answer the question I'd been asking myself since I was a child – did I have any acting talent?

Short answer?

I didn't.

Back in the day, City Lit acting classes were so popular – and still are! – that people would start queuing up the night before enrolment opened to ensure a place on the course. In the present day that's no longer necessary but in the 1980s it was definitely a thing. I didn't know this, so I turned up on the day of enrolment to find all the places on every evening or weekend drama course had already been snapped up. I was determined not to make the same mistake again. The following year, I joined the queue the night before enrolment day. I took my groundsheet and sleeping bag and flask of coffee. I was all set. My partner Neil didn't like the idea of me staying out all night, possibly sleeping round the back of the building where the alleyway was narrow and dark, so he came with me. He sat on the groundsheet all night like a faithful guard dog, his expression thunderous. He was not happy. Neither Neil nor I are camping folk. I love the great outdoors, but at night I'm happy to view it from a comfy bed and with an adjacent bathroom with functioning indoor plumbing. That night outside the City Lit I was in a great mood because I was close enough to the front of the queue to ensure I at least got considered for a place on an acting course.

The following morning, the moment the City Lit doors opened, Neil was out of there. I received my ticket with the time I would be seen and was on cloud nine. A white woman in her twenties saw my ticket and asked me to give it to her as she'd only just turned up and didn't realise that people queued overnight to get on the acting courses.

'Please can I have it,' she pleaded. 'I really want to get on an acting course and be an actress.'

'So do I,' I replied.

She looked me up and down. 'I stand more chance than you. Please can I have your ticket?'

I looked her up and down and thought to myself, 'Bitch, please!'

She might stand more chance than me, but I would stand no chance at all if I didn't try. And she'd pissed me off with her assumption that I would just give up the ticket that I'd spent all night queuing for simply because she asked for it. I went to the designated area to wait to be called, leaving the wannabe actress begging more people in the foyer for their tickets.

At last it was my turn. I was interviewed and accepted on the course. I was in!

The drama course was excellent and blasted me well and truly out of my comfort zone, which is always a good thing. Movement, voice, creating characters – I loved all of those elements. Even though some of the voice exercises made me feel a bit daft, I told myself that we were all doing them and I had to get over myself. I loved it all – except the actual acting! Any time we did improvisations, my heart would beat like the Nicholas Brothers' feet, so much so that I was convinced I was going to have a heart attack. The course tutor would give us different scenarios to improvise around. Now, don't get me wrong, I loved coming up with ideas and stories around the brief we were given. I enjoyed collaborating with others and *loved* making up the scenes that we would then act out. But actually standing up in front of the rest of the class and acting? As my sister would say, 'Nah, sir.' When our tutor Valerie asked, 'OK, friends, who wants to go next?' the hands of everyone – and I mean everyone – in the class would shoot up. Except mine. I used to sink into my chair, trying to make myself as small as possible and I'd genuinely feel sick.

But I'd do it.

I would stand up and act.

And it proved to me that I *could* do it. It showed me that I could stand up in front of others and be looked at and watched – and not die! By the end of the year, however, I'd decided that, though I loved the course, acting was not for me. This was further confirmed when one of the course tutors took me to one said and said, 'Lorie, I've noticed you come up with some really great ideas. Have you ever thought of writing them down and doing something with them?'

'I used to write stories and poems. I still do, occasionally,' I admitted.

'Well, maybe you could get something published,' said the tutor. At my look of surprise, she smiled. 'Just think about it. And there are several excellent writing courses here at the City Lit.'

I did think about it. A lot. Until it was the only thing I could think about.

I'd been writing stories and poems for my own amusement

since I was eight or nine. I wrote a lot as a teen, mostly poems as an emotional outlet, but some fictional stories too. Why hadn't I considered writing classes before? By that time I'd devoured the works of a number of Black writers, mostly African American but also a number of novels from Caribbean and African authors. However, the only Black authors I'd found who were born or permanently lived in Britain were James Berry, Grace Nichols, John Agard and Benjamin Zephaniah and their books were all poetry collections. Don't get me wrong, their poetry was amazing and truly cemented my love of the form, but I wanted to write stories in prose. Did UK publishers even publish fictional stories by Black authors born and raised in Britain? I hadn't come across any . . . but I decided I wasn't going to let that stop me.

Time to sign up for some writing classes.

33

The idea of writing stories and getting them published took root and flourished, but the problem was I had zero clue about the publishing world. I joined a 'Ways Into Writing' workshop run by Carole Burns. And I loved it. Her evening classes were the highlight of my week. She would give us exercises to do in the class, which I relished, but was too shy to read out what I wrote. She would also give us homework and ask us to bring in our writing the following week. I always did it – usually on the same night it was set – and brought it to class for the next lesson. Most weeks, Carole would ask, 'Lorie, would you like to read it out for us?' And I'd always reply, 'Not today, Carole.' She put up with this for the first term, but by the time we were well into the second, I could see that her patience with me was evaporating.

'Lorie, do you want to be a writer?' she asked, exasperated after yet another refusal from me to read out my homework.

'More than anything else in the world,' I replied sincerely.

'Then you need to shit or get off the pot!'

The class erupted with laughter. I laughed too, though I was totally mortified.

But she was absolutely right. It really was one of the best pieces of advice I've ever received, and I've applied it to all aspects of my life ever since. If I'm asked to attend an event or take part in something and I say yes, then I'm going to go for it.

Don't faff around umming and ahing, just do it – and do it properly. No half-arse efforts!

Carole gave me a life lesson in the moment when I needed it

most. After that, whenever she invited me to read out my work, I never declined.

Once the 'Ways Into Writing' course had finished, I was thirsty to learn more. I signed up for as many City Lit evening courses as I could – a women writers' workshop, playwriting, science fiction writing, short story writing. I also signed up for a comedy writing course and a thriller writing course at other venues. I bought every how-to-write book I could find. I wasn't mucking about! And I devoured them all. My philosophy regarding my writing was 'go hard or go home'. It wasn't just that I wanted to be an author, I *needed* to be one. If I wanted to be taken seriously, I had to take writing seriously – and that meant research. With that in mind, my how-to collection grew and grew: how to write for children, for television, for radio; how to write thrillers, screenplays, mysteries, romances, science fiction, historical fiction, horror, suspense novels, short stories. I also bought writers' guides on poisons, police procedures, forensic medicine, crimes of deception, crime scene investigations, private investigators, criminal psychology and weaponry. I ate, drank, slept and breathed stories. When I wasn't reading, I was writing.

But I still wasn't sure *what* I wanted to write. What genre and for what audience?

One day I finished a Mills and Boon novel which was decidedly subpar. At the end of the story was a note from the editors which began as follows:

Hello!

You've come to the end of this story and we truly hope that
    you enjoyed it.

If you did (or even if you didn't!), have you ever thought that
    you might like to try writing a romance yourself?

Well, I hadn't until I read the note from the editors. They were actively looking for new authors and invited those interested to write to them with a self-addressed envelope for a copy of their guidelines. I sent off for them, read them carefully when they arrived, then started writing.

Several weeks later I had written my first adult novel, called *Fool Me Twice*. My hero and heroine were both Black. I described their ebony hair and facial features in detail, but I didn't explicitly state their skin colour. At the time, I'd never read a Mills and Boon romance that featured a Black hero or heroine. However, that wasn't going to stop me – I just wanted to see if I could write one. Besides, Mills and Boon were actively looking for authors, so why not me?

Once I'd finished writing my story and had checked it for typos, I sent it to the address specified, which was in Brooks Mews, London. Weeks later, to my delight, I was invited to the Mills and Boon offices to discuss my book. Their letter told me that it wasn't quite right for their list but they'd like to discuss it with me. Hopeful that they might give me pointers on how to edit it so that it was publishable, I said yes to a meeting. On the day in question, I arrived bright and early (I try to be scrupulous about not being late to any appointment) and I was taken to a room to meet two female editors, one of whom was called Mary. She introduced herself as a senior commissioning editor. We had a chat about my story, which had too many flaws to be redeemable, but Mary told me she'd be happy to see any more stories that I wanted to send them.

That encouragement was everything.

I left their office full of enthusiasm and ready to write another romance. However, the second attempt was much harder than the first for the simple reason that my heart wasn't truly in it. I'm not disparaging romances – on the contrary, I love to read them when I'm in the mood – but somehow I felt a bit of a fraud as I was writing the second one. I realised that it was easier for a camel to pass through the eye of a needle than for a feminist to write about alpha males as the kind of men that women should aspire to marry.

But thanks to Mills and Boon, I started on my journey towards becoming an author. The trouble was, I felt no closer to homing in on what I did want to write about.

One day, as I was on my way to the City Lit for my playwriting course, I popped into the Puffin Bookshop in Covent Garden as I had some time to kill. It had been quite a while since I'd been around the children's section in a library or a bookshop and I was keen to see just how much more diverse the selection would be compared to my childhood. I walked around and I looked and I searched and I practically lost my eyesight trying to find a Black child – any Black child – on a book jacket.

There wasn't one.

Thinking I had to be wrong and was just not looking in the right place, I asked one of the booksellers at the till.

'We don't have any,' came the reply.

We don't have any. Seriously?

I left the bookshop and headed for the City Lit, deep in thought. Why had nothing changed since my childhood? Why were there still no books that featured Black children? Over the next few weeks, I popped into the Puffin Bookshop every week on my way to the City Lit. I started buying children's books again, wanting to find out what new topics and themes were being tackled. The tone of the books had definitely changed. They were faster paced and less priggish, but they seemed to be targeted at a junior school audience with very little for the young adult market. That hadn't changed much, then. And children of colour were practically non-existent within them. That hadn't changed much either. The odd playground or group illustration might have a Black child somewhere in the background, but that was it.

Well, hell no! Maybe I could write a book for children that would have a Black protagonist and have a Black child on the cover. Maybe I could try to write all the books I would've loved to read as a child. Books that would've welcomed me into the world of literature and reassured me that I wasn't alone. I signed up for a beginner's 'Writing for Children' class just to get a flavour of what would be involved. The course tutor was the phenomenal Elizabeth Hawkins, one of the best tutors I've ever had.

Midway through the first term, every writing gear in my head clicked into place. I knew I had found the target audience for my stories. Children and teens are intelligent, discerning and brutally honest. Just what I wanted. Plus, I reasoned there would be less innate prejudice in reading books by a Black author from children of a different background to mine if I could just grab them with the story. If I wrote for children, I could write across a number of different interests, age ranges and genres. I wouldn't have to change my name if I changed genre – a situation authors regularly came up against when writing for adults. Elizabeth also told us that the consensus within the children's publishing world seemed to be that children's books may not sell as many copies initially, but they had a longevity that many books written for adults did not. Adult books tended to have one year, two at most, to prove themselves. Children's books ticked along for far longer before going out of print. As far as I was concerned, writing stories for children was mostly positives and very few negatives. But among the latter was the huge one that UK publishers didn't seem to publish stories by UK-based Black authors.

I made up my mind. I was going to be an author. This wasn't going to be a hobby or a pastime but a long-term, lifetime career.

Elizabeth's first course ran for three terms, each with a different focus regarding the age range of the target reader. In the autumn term we studied the form and format of picture books and tried to write our own; the spring term was dedicated to early readers (books for the five-plus age range); and in the summer term we explored writing for an older age range (books for nine-plus). This was before YA books were the huge part of the market they are today. I really enjoyed each term and truly believe it was this foundation year that made me want to write across the various age ranges. Each age range came with its own set of rules and guidelines and I enjoyed the discipline of creating stories that worked for particular ranges or across ranges. In Elizabeth's workshop class, which I joined the following autumn, we would bring in our writing each week for feedback. I attended her workshop courses for four or five years, even after becoming a published author, and *loved* them.

Elizabeth had a very clever method for making us really dissect our writing submissions. She would never let us read our own work to the group. Our stories had to be brought in typed up and double spaced, then handed over to someone else to read. And oh my God but the process was instructive – and sometimes painful. Having our writing read out loud by someone else was an excellent indicator of what was working and what wasn't. Any stumbles or fumbles in the reading usually indicated that the text required simplifying or clarifying. If the reader didn't understand what he or she was reading, it became evident rapidly. Even today, once I've finished a chapter that requires further work, I will at the very least record myself reading it and then listen to the playback a day or two later. Then it feels as if someone else is narrating a story and it allows me to be more objective. Of course, it's even better to let someone else read and record it and then to listen to the playback. When you read your own work, you know where the inflections and the emotions should be emphasised and will read it accordingly. It's instructive to have someone else read and record it at the same time, as they will be coming to the text fresh.

Another effective practice that Elizabeth employed was to tell the person whose work was being read that they were not allowed to speak until everyone in the class had finished critiquing their work. Oh, the pain! But it was a necessary part of the process. It was and still is so exposing to share your stories when they're a work in progress. You feel incredibly vulnerable. The instinct for all authors who hear criticism of their work is to leap in and defend their baby.

No, you misunderstood—

You're misinterpreting what I meant—

My character never said/meant/did/thought (delete as appropriate) that—

Justifications and excuses are easy to grab for when your baby is being maligned. Which was exactly why the author having their work read out wasn't allowed to speak – because for most of us, when we're speaking, we're no longer listening. Elizabeth's point of view was that we had to listen to the criticism even if we deemed it wrong, because if more than one person said the same thing, well, maybe the fault wasn't with them but with our writing.

Now, I admit, occasionally I disagreed with the consensus, but most of the time I didn't. Because of the size of the class, not everyone had the chance to have their work read out every week. I tended to bring in chapters that were proving problematic and I was not alone in that. The person having their work read out was allowed to summarise the plot up until the chapter to be read, but that was all. No other explanations, prevarications or equivocations were allowed. This meant that if a plot point in a particular chapter proved to be confusing for the others in the class, I could take the criticism on board and make sure to address it. Stories must have a life of their own and stand on their own feet. The author can't be with each reader, standing over their shoulder and explaining the characters' motivations, the plot points, the intricacies of theme and setting. It was another salutary lesson to learn.

I remember a time I took a horror story into class to be read out. This was after I'd already had a couple of books published. The story was about a boy in a psychiatric ward of a hospital who kept having flashbacks about his twin brother attacking him. At the end of the reading, the class was split down the middle between those who loved it and those who thought it was too horrific for teens to read. I must admit, I listened gleefully as the class debated the story and whether it should be toned down or left alone. When I garnered that reaction I knew I had something. That something turned into my book *Jon For Short* (published by Barrington Stoke, illustrated by Vladimir Stankovic). The fact is I write the books I would've loved to read as a child and a teen. That's always my starting point – does this subject matter interest me? If it doesn't, I can't write about it.

Attending Elizabeth's class taught me so much. I gained a true appreciation of the hard work required to craft a book for children and I learned a lot about the children's publishing world. I also spent time with other would-be authors as well as some who had already been published. Every time someone had a book accepted by a publisher, it was cele-brated as if we had all succeeded. To be honest, it felt like a victory for everyone in the class. When I was struggling to get published, I remember being so happy for those who'd had their books accepted for publication – especially if it was a project they'd brought to class and we'd watched as they developed and honed the story – but I would also wistfully promise myself that, one day, I too would have something accepted for publication. One day.

I will be forever grateful that I stumbled across Elizabeth's class and indeed the City Lit when I did. They say, 'What's for you, won't go by you'. I'm not sure that's entirely true. I think you have to look out for opportunities and throw yourself on them like a wrestler when they appear. I've attended any number of writing classes with writers far more talented than me, but they'd get one or two rejection letters and then we'd never see them again.

That was never going to be me.

All my life I've been accused of being incredibly stubborn – which is true.

There are occasions when negative traits can lead to posi-tive outcomes.

Negative	Positive
I'm stubborn	I never give up
I'm impatient	I get things done
I get too emotional	I'm empathetic
I have a short fuse	I rant and then it's over
I remember the past vividly	I remember the past vividly
I can recall conversations by heart	I can recall conversations by heart

Remembering the past vividly and recalling conversations verbatim are both a blessing and a curse. Bad days play on my mind like they happened yesterday, but, on the plus side, the good days do the same. I don't recall all conversations but the ones that stand out tend to stand out for years.

Anyway, I'd finally settled on what kind of stories I wanted to tell and decided on my intended audience – and I threw myself into it with passion. Every spare waking moment was spent writing. Each year I bought the *Writers' Handbook* and the *Writers' and Artists' Yearbook* and studied them carefully regarding children's publishers. These publications gave the names, addresses and submission details of UK publishers and agents. They were a valuable resource in my efforts to know as much as possible about the world I wanted to be a part of. I wanted to know the names of the managing directors, the senior commissioning editors, what kind of stories they were looking for. I also subscribed to *The Bookseller*, a weekly magazine aimed at those in the publishing industry. It covered anything and everything to do with books. *The Bookseller* kept me informed of which editors were moving to other publishing houses and what was going on in the book world from week to week.

Shopping trips consisted of buying the essentials then heading straight for the nearest bookshop to see who was publishing what. When I wasn't writing, I was reading – and absorbing. That was my life.

After proper research, I'd send out the picture books and early readers I'd written – but without fail, they all got bounced back to me. The standard phrase was 'not suitable for our list'. A polite way of letting would-be authors down gently. The moment I sent off a story to a publisher, I'd start working on my next project. That way I could tell myself if a number of publishers all rejected my previous story, well maybe, just maybe, one of them might take the next one. Each story was sent to at least seven or eight publishers, usually the bigger players like Penguin and HarperCollins, as I reasoned that they published so many books each year, surely they could find room for one of mine? I learned later that, ironically, bigger publishing houses are less likely not more likely to take on an unknown author. It's the smaller independent publishers who are more prepared to take a chance with a debut writer.

After sending out a story for consideration, the following weeks were filled with optimism and hope. That's what kept me going. Occasionally editors' letters accompanied my returned manuscript telling me *why* my story was unsuitable, which I took as a good sign. If an editor was taking the time and trouble to tell me in detail why my story didn't work, then surely they must see something in my writing worth encouraging? That's what I told myself. However, I kept writing picture books and early readers and the rejection letters kept on coming for a year and several months. By this time the rejections numbered in the high sixties. I felt sure that I'd sent at least one of my stories to practically every children's book publisher based in London. Was I deluding myself? Maybe I'd never get published. The thing of it is, I not only wanted but *needed* to be an author. It felt like not just a natural outlet but the only outlet for my voice, for the stories I wanted to share, the ideas I wanted to communicate.

And I wanted to get paid for it.

First rule of writing stories – you can't publish what you haven't written. The science of writing stories begins with the application of bum to chair and fingers to pen or keyboard. So even when I had a full-time job, I wrote. Every spare moment was spent typing. The ticks of the clock belonged to my job in computing. I lived for the spaces between the ticks. That was my time. But it wasn't enough. My job was getting in the way, but I simply couldn't afford to give it up. Thou shalt pay bills. That became my mum's eleventh commandment when she and my dad separated. She always said that even if she didn't eat, she would make sure her rent and all the utility bills were paid. That money ethic rubbed off on me. There was no way I would ever let myself get into serious debt, not if I could help it. As a consequence, I inevitably grew to resent any time away from home and my computer. But what could I do?

34

It was 1989 and I kept on writing but still no publisher was biting. I was in the region of my seventieth rejection letter and unwelcome doubts were starting to take root. That's when I read in a newspaper that Alice Walker was coming to visit the UK to promote her latest book, *The Temple of My Familiar.* I could hardly believe it.

Alice Walker was coming!

My excitement was off the scale. I *needed* to meet her. Here's why.

One Friday evening in January 1984, I was strolling along Upper Street in Islington on my way to the cinema to see Stephen King's *The Dead Zone*, when I came across the Black Bookshop. Now I don't know if that was its real name on the signage above the door, but I do remember that the window was full of books, most of which had Black people on the covers. Naturally, I went in! And it was like being back at the dentist and floating upwards all over again. The shop was full of books written by or about Black people. Most of the authors were from America, Africa or the Caribbean. Very few were British. The shelves contained fiction to the left and non-fiction to the right and I stood in the middle of the shop in awed amazement at the books all around me. I felt like I had grown considerably taller just by being in that space. Because I didn't want to miss the beginning of my film, I did a quick recce, then decided to buy a number of history books about Black people I'd never heard of before: Olaudah

Equiano, Mary Seacole, Toussaint Louverture and Nanny of the Maroons. And I bought one novel called *The Color Purple* by Alice Walker.

When I was at secondary school and we had to choose our O-level subjects, one of the first I dropped was history. As far as I was concerned it was boring and, more than that, irrelevant. We never learned about working-class people and how they lived, we didn't learn about the causes of the World Wars, the reasons for the strife between Britain and Ireland or anything else that would've been useful and interesting. It was all kings and queens – mostly Henry VIII ad nauseam. When I was twelve and in Year 7, I once asked my history teacher, Mrs M, why we never learned about Black scientists and pioneers and inventors.

'Because there aren't any,' she said with disdain.

I was sure that couldn't be true, but I'd certainly never read about or been taught about any, so how could I refute what she'd said? That's why on that first day in the Black Bookshop, I bought so many non-fiction books, particularly history books, and my eyes were opened to the truth. Here were facts about Black scientists, inventors, achievers – the very people my history teacher told me didn't exist. They existed – not only in America but in Britain, the Caribbean and Africa too – but their accomplishments were not spoken about. Worse than that, their endeavours and triumphs, their very lives were erased. Whitewashed. Black British men and women of note were deliberately excluded from the British history books. It seemed to me that to concede that British history wasn't just white history was to shine a spotlight on our *true* history – all of it. Wilberforce is taught; Olaudah Equiano is not. The abolition of slavery is studied; the centuries of slave trade and ownership that made Britain incredibly wealthy and laid the bloody foundation for the British Empire were conveniently forgotten in all the history books I was taught from.

In your face, Mrs M!

The following day, I sat down with *The Color Purple* and read it in one go. It was the very first novel I read written by a Black author featuring Black protagonists, and it had a profound effect on me – not just the story itself, but the fact of who wrote it. Alice Walker opened a door onto the world of the literary possible. She was a Black woman author. They existed! I read the other books I'd bought and then, as soon as I could, headed back to the bookshop in Upper Street. That was where and how I discovered Toni Morrison, Buchi Emecheta, Rosa Guy, Ntozake Shange, Walter Mosley and a host of others.

So when, five years later, I heard that Alice Walker was coming to the UK for a book tour, best believe I researched if, when and where she was coming to my area. As far as I was concerned, anywhere in London was my area. As a south Londoner, travelling anywhere north of the Thames gave me a nosebleed, but if it would take me three hours to get to whatever bookshop she was at, then so be it. Alice Walker had enriched my world and I really wanted to meet her. It turns out I didn't need to travel quite so far.

I found out she would be at Silver Moon Bookshop on Charing Cross Road on 22 September 1989. On the day in question, I rocked up bright and early. Unfortunately, so did the hundreds of others who wanted to get their books signed. The queue stretched out for what felt like a mile. I joined at the back and waited – and moved slowly forward. And waited some more. I would've waited all night if I had to. There was something about Alice Walker's writing that spoke to me. As far as I was concerned, she wrote the truth – warts, fresh scars, and deep gaping wounds and all. But she also wrote about the beauty, the resilience, the resourcefulness, forbearance and everyday joys of normal people.

After almost three hours, it was finally my turn to get her latest book *The Temple of My Familiar* signed. Alice sat behind a wooden desk. She wore round glasses that in no way diminished her fiercely intelligent eyes, and her ebony locks reached down to her shoulders.

'Please could you write "don't give up" in it for me?' I requested.

'I can't write that. What does that mean?' asked Alice Walker.

'Well, I want to be a writer more than anything else in the world, but I keep getting rejection letters. I've had over seventy now,' I explained.

She looked me in the eye, pointing her pen at me. 'Don't give up,' she ordered with a smile.

And that's what she wrote in my book. I walked back to Charing Cross train station, clutching my signed book to my chest, a ridiculous grin on my face all the way home. I couldn't give up on my dream to be an author now. Alice Walker had told me not to! At my lowest ebb, Alice Walker's words kept me going.

Over the years, I've sometimes told this story at literary events. In the book signings afterwards, I have frequently been asked to write the same thing in the books of aspiring writers. I'm more than happy to do so. And I hope the words inspire all the aspiring writers the way they inspired me.

35

Oh, the irony! I'd spent my life as a misfit, being ridiculed or mockingly indulged for seeing the world differently to everyone else, but, to my delighted amazement, this was my major asset when writing. Even though I had yet to be published, my writing tutors and the others in my writing classes never derided my imagination, nor how it manifested in my stories. In fact, just the opposite. More than one tutor had commented on my original vision and writing style.

I was once asked – after two decades of being a full-time author – how I would describe my own writing. That's an easy one. I'm a storyteller who tells her stories on the page rather than out loud. If you're looking for lyrical, evocative language, if you're seeking a master lexicographer who will never use one word where twenty-five will do, if you're seeking a writer who will have you rushing to the dictionary after every paragraph, then don't go looking in my books! Quite frankly, I'm rubbish at telling jokes or stories in conversation. I'm the sort of person who will tell a joke and put the punchline in the wrong place, or who will miss an important point that makes the joke funny. But I found having my own way of viewing the world, my own way of describing things, having a logical way of plotting stories (as opposed to the circular thinking often required for jokes) actually worked in my favour when writing.

The desire for order and logic means that I'm very pedantic or overly literal, and I used to be terrible for correcting people when they got things factually wrong. Contrarily and perhaps counterintuitively, my imagination meant I could take an object and fill it with a purpose and/or meaning that others just couldn't see. Once, in Year 6 of primary school, our teacher held up a tennis racket and asked us to write down all the things we could use it for. Most people wrote down 'play tennis' and then stopped. A couple of people wrote down, 'use it as a snowshoe' and then stopped. I filled the page with all the things I would use it for – playing tennis, one snowshoe, straining fat spaghetti, using it as a doily to decorate an enormous cake, draping scarves and flowers around it to wear as a jaunty hat, wearing it as a brace along my back to help me sit up straight, using it as a bridge with many routes for insects to cross a narrow stream or river – you get the idea.

Round about the time of receiving my sixtieth rejection letter, something strange began to happen. I started having terrifying nightmares. Dreams so horrific that I would end up kicking out and clawing and screaming myself awake, eyes saucer-wide with terror. The nightmares occurred so often that they began to paint darkened circles beneath my eyes, and regularly interrupted sleep had me overtired during the day. My work was beginning to suffer. My resentment for the job that was keeping me fed and was paying my mortgage wasn't abating. Basically, my head was in turmoil. My life from the outside looked perfect. Let's face it, my life from the inside could've been a helluva lot worse.

But it wasn't enough.

Days turned into weeks and I was still having debilitating nightmares, which were growing more frequent. After the fifth or sixth bad dream, I started sleeping with a notepad and pen beside my bed so that I could record them in as much detail as possible whenever they woke me up. After a couple of months, I had quite a collection, ranging from a sentence or two to whole pages. Here are just two nightmares I remember particularly vividly:

I am alone during the day and working at my computer in a back bedroom, when I hear the sound of my front door being kicked in. What the hell? I run out onto the landing and look down the stairs to see two men standing in my hall, each wearing a motorcycle visor and holding a gun. They are here for me, to kill me. As they glance up, I jerk backwards, my heart racing. They haven't seen me, have they? I listen as they enter the living room at the front of the house.

What should I do?

They come out of the living room and head for the kitchen. I creep quickly down the stairs, hoping to make a dash for it through the busted-open door. But then I hear footsteps heading towards me. If I try to make a run for it now, I'll get a bullet in my back. I run into the living room, crouching behind an armchair.

'They've already checked in here,' I tell myself, trying not to panic, forcing myself to think rationally. 'When they head upstairs searching for you, make a run for it.'

I hear footsteps start upstairs, but only one pair of footsteps. Where is the other man? In the hall? I hold my breath, terrified that the men will hear my gasps for breath or my heart trying to punch its way out of my chest.

All at once, the armchair is pulled to one side. One of the men stands before me, his gun pointing straight at me. He raises his visor, smiles and shouts, 'Unemployed.'

Then he shoots me through the forehead.

Instantly my body goes icy cold. My vision turns blindingly white, a white so bright like nothing I've ever seen before.

I am dying. Before the very last moment of my life, I wake up screaming.

It feels like if I'd left it just one more second, I would've died in my sleep.

The second dream:

I'm in a forest all by myself, wearing a black leather jacket, a worn black woollen jumper, denim jeans and black boots. To my horror, I feel a single drop of rain fall against my cheek. I brush it off at once, trying not to panic. The drop feels like a needle has been thrust into my skin. The rain is not just acidic but deadly. Another drop falls on the shoulder of my jacket and immediately eats a hole into it. I need to find shelter. Fast. Up ahead, in the distance, I see a light through the trees. Shelter. I race towards it, dodging around tree trunks and leaping over shrubs as the raindrops fall faster. I reach a clearing in which sits a picture-book house – a solid wooden door in the middle, with bay windows on either side of it on the ground and first floors. Warm, welcoming yellow light floods out from the windows. Sanctuary. I run to the front door and try to push it open but it is locked against me. I bang on the door over and over until the bones in my hand must surely break. At the windows on either side of me people start to appear. White people. Mostly women.

'Let me in! Please let me in. It's raining. Please.'

But the people stand at the windows watching me, their faces expressionless.

'Please. I'll die out here if you don't let me in,' I beg.

No one moves. No one speaks.

The rain is falling harder now. It lashes at my cheeks. I wipe my face. Strips of skin fall onto my hands only to be washed away and dissolved by the rain.

The pain I feel is lacerating.

These people are going to watch me die, I realise as I sink to the ground, unable to stand any longer.

And still the people watch.
I scream out in frustration, one last defiant shriek at death itself.
One last scream that wakes me up.

I didn't need to be a psychiatrist to understand most of the dreams. I hated my job but was terrified of being unemployed. And the acid-rain dream? Years later, I realised what that one meant too. The house in the clearing was the world of publishing. The acid rain falling on me was my life if I stayed in computing. That world was eating away at me and would've continued to do so until there was nothing left. In my nightmare, the white people at the bay windows – mostly women – were all the editors and editorial readers who kept sending me rejection letter after rejection letter.

Nightmares were still coming at me night after night. It occurred to me that maybe I could do something with them. I reasoned that if I turned them into stories, then I could take control of them, rather than the dreams taking control of me. This carried on for a few months with me growing more and more miserable, until my partner Neil and I sat down one day to discuss what we could do about it. I couldn't go on the way I had been doing. I needed to do something different as my rejection letters now numbered in the lower seventies. All my picture books and early reader stories were being returned one after the other by different publishers, some with the standard 'not suitable for our list' letter, some with more detailed explanations as to why they were being rejected. The bottom line was no one wanted to publish them.

Unwelcome doubts were beginning to creep into my head. If all the editors at all the different publishing houses were saying no, shouldn't I listen? Maybe some of my friends and family were right when they said that I was wasting my time because publishers in Britain would never publish stories by a Black British writer.

But I couldn't give up. Not when I wanted so badly to be a published author.

I was a woman on a mission.

36

Working in computing had begun to take a mental toll around my umptieth rejection letter. Every Friday night I would be euphorically happy. Weirdly, freakishly so. Leaving the office on a Friday evening had me feeling invincible, unstoppable. But each Sunday evening was a different story. There'd always be something wrong with me – a migraine, lower backaches, upper chest pains, joint issues, abdominal woes. These were ailments that hit me hard. On top of that, I'd feel so down, so wretchedly miserable that it was a struggle to even get out of bed on Monday morning.

It took me far too long to realise that my infirmities were psychosomatic. Friday evenings came with a promise of a whole weekend of writing. Sunday afternoons arrived with the prospect of a week doing a job that I no longer cared about and which was solely a means to an end. I prided myself on being too much of a professional to half-arse it, but I grew to hate my job, the commute, all of it. People – including me – pushing and shoving to get on a train, then shoving and pushing some more to get off it again. I was sick and tired of commuters who were prepared to knock me down and run me over just so they could be at work five minutes earlier. And for the longest while, I'd been just like them. So caught up and entrenched in the rat race that I couldn't even see that I was a part of it.

The aches and pains I was going through, as well as the regular nightmares that were plaguing me, were a physical manifestation of the mess my mind was in. It was my mind and body joining forces to tell me that they didn't want to work in computing any more! Something had to give. Neil and I scrutinised old bills, made projections of forthcoming expenditure and worked out our finances for the next several months. After careful consideration we calculated that we could afford for me to give up my job to write full-time, with Neil picking up the slack and paying all the bills – but only for one year. If I made a good go of writing, then I could carry on with it for as long as we could pay our bills. However, if I hadn't sold any books in that time then it would be back to full-time employment in computing. The moment the decision was made, I knew how Atlas felt when Hercules took over from him. A huge burden had been lifted from my shoulders.

The plan was to carry on working for a few months to save some money, and then I could hand in my notice. I wrote every evening and well into the night and saved my money like a pre-Christmas Ebenezer Scrooge. No more eating out, no more takeaway meals, no more clothes shopping (which I hated doing anyway), no more holidays, no more running the washing machine on half loads, no more lights left on in empty rooms. I saved every spare penny and wrote in the evenings. And saved some more. And wrote well into the night. And saved. And received more rejection letters.

One piece of advice that neophyte authors invariably get is 'write what you know'. I don't agree with this advice if it's used as a stick to prod authors back into their lane, but it is a legitimate starting point. I knew nightmares from the ones I'd been regularly having and recording in the notepad I kept on my bedside table. One day, as I was reading through them, it occurred to me that some were really nasty and would make great short stories. I picked the most terrifying ones, created plots around them and sat down to write. The stories poured out of me. It was a case of the tales pulling me along, rather than me having to push them to get them moving. As these were definitely not for a younger age range, I started researching where I might send them once I'd finished writing them. At the time, very few publishers had lists that catered for teenagers, so the choice was extremely limited.

I wrote sixteen stories, recorded myself reading them, played them back, edited them, gave them to my partner to read, edited them some more, reworked, re-edited and re-crafted until I really felt I couldn't do any more to them without professional feedback. Then off they went with a stamped addressed envelope to Livewire Books for Teenagers, which was an imprint of the now sadly defunct publisher The Women's Press.

And I waited. After a month I received a letter.

Dear Malorie Blackman,

Thank you for sending us your short story collection, Not So Stupid! *We would love to publish your stories in an anthology for teens.*

After a scream of delight, came another and another.

At last!

After eighty-two rejection letters, a publisher had finally said yes. The vinyl 12-inch of the McFadden & Whitehead hit song 'Ain't No Stopping Us Now' didn't come off my record turntable for the rest of the day! All those years of classes and workshops, all the books I'd read on writing, all those dreams and schemes, cutbacks and sacrifices had finally paid off. I could now call myself a published writer.

The day I received that letter was one of the very best of my life. I was invited to The Women's Press offices to speak to Carole Spedding, who would be my editor. We got on so well and she seemed to understand me and my writing. We discussed which parts of what stories would need reworking, which I did with a happy heart. Once I had finished working on my short story collection, a publication date was set – 1 November 1990. In the meantime, I started working on my next book, a picture book called *Wendy's New Dress*. I sent it off to two publishers at once. To my delight and chagrin, both wrote to me offering to publish it. After years of having my picture books rejected, here were two publishers who wanted the same book. Maybe it helped that I could now say that I was a soon-to-be published author. Or maybe my writing had improved noticeably during the rejection-letter years. Whatever the reason, it was flattering to have two publishers offering for the same story. I went with the publisher whose letter arrived first, Simon & Schuster, even though the second publisher offered more money. The title of the book was changed to *That New Dress*. When my third book, an early reader, was accepted for publication – but before any of the three titles had hit the bookshops – I submitted my resignation. It wasn't a hard decision. Now that I had three offers from three different publishers, I also found an agent prepared to take me on. That was such a relief, as more and more publishers were beginning to insist on manuscripts being submitted by agents only. Getting an agent felt like a verification and validation of my dreams for the future.

I was going to be a full-time writer.

My last day as a database manager was Friday, 2 November 1990. No more company car. No more business trips abroad. No more workplace perks. No more great salary.

Saturday, 3 November was my first day of being self-employed, and it was scary.

And exciting.

And oh so wonderful.

It felt like my life had begun again, bright and shiny and buzzing with potential and possibilities.

In my first year of writing, I wrote and sold another book, called *Elaine, You're a Brat*. I made just over eight hundred pounds for the whole year. Repeat – eight hundred pounds for *the whole year*. But I was a full-time author; no more commute to work, no more bosses to report to, no more permission needed for holidays, no more doctor's letter required when I was ill. And no more waking up to dread each working day. I was now my own boss, could set my own hours and I was doing something I loved.

It was one of the happiest years of my life.

37

During my first year as a full-time writer, I started working on my first novel, *Hacker*. The picture books and early readers were fun to write but I was ready for the challenge of writing a full-length novel. What should I write about? Well, I knew computing, so wouldn't it make sense to base my story around computers? How about a story about someone who, while using their computer, somehow manages to swap personalities with it? My heroine could become cold and brutally analytical, while her true personality would somehow manifest itself within the processing core of her computer. The idea – and that's all it was – felt like it might have possibilities, so I sat down at my computer, typed 'HACKER', and began – with no plot plan, no character outlines, no story arc. I just wanted to write to see where my brain and fingers would take me.

Eight months of crazy hard slog later, I had written a 250-page, 50,000-words-long novel about a girl called Robyn who loses her humanity due to an accident with her computer, and about her brother's struggle to somehow get his true sister back. My very first novel! I checked it for typos and off it went. Transworld Publishers wrote back to me and invited me to an editorial meeting to discuss my book.

I thought – 'YES! I'M IN!'

On the agreed date, off I went to the meeting with high hopes and dreaming of how the cover might work, the marketing plans, how I might publicise it – all those good things. In that meeting I met the woman who was to be my editor for more than two decades, Annie Eaton, and the one and only David Fickling who was a senior commissioning editor at Transworld at the time. After all the pleasantries had been concluded, we got down to discussing my book. This is how I remember it. Annie insists to this day that it wasn't quite this brutal!

'We love your writing and feel you really have a strong voice. However, we felt the ending of your story didn't quite work.'

'Well, no worries. I'm here to learn and I can fix any problems,' I thought with confidence.

I made copious notes while Annie told me why the ending didn't quite work.

'We felt the beginning wasn't quite right.'

Hmm . . . I made more copious notes as it was explained to me why the beginning wasn't quite right.

'We felt you needed to work on the middle a bit more.'

By this point, I was still making notes but I was starting to wonder why on earth they'd invited me in to discuss a book that obviously just wasn't working. At the end of the meeting, I thanked them for their time and consideration and told them that I would get to work on the rewrites the moment I got home. Which wasn't strictly true. I went home and had another read of the manuscript. It had been a couple of months between sending it out and my meeting with Annie and David, so I could now read my story with more objectivity.

And guess what? They were absolutely right. There were more holes in the plot than in a pair of net curtains. Even though it broke my heart, I took all 250 pages of my manuscript and dumped the whole lot in the bin. Then I sat down to start again from scratch. I kept the title, because that's the only thing Annie and David hadn't mentioned, and I wrote a synopsis of what the new plot might be:

One day Vicki Gibson and her brother Richard (everyone calls him Gib) come home from school to be told that their dad has been arrested for embezzling money from the bank where he works. One million pounds was found in their dad's bank account. They know their dad isn't a thief so they hack into the bank's computer to try and find out who took the money. Why would the real thief go to the trouble of transferring all that money into their dad's account and not their own?

Now, here's the thing: it would've been easy when I came out of the meeting to give up, to think, 'Obviously writing novels is not for me.' But that never for a single moment entered my mind. I was grateful for the feedback and appreciated the fact that they wouldn't have wasted their time inviting me in to talk about my novel if they felt I couldn't write for love nor money. Of course I was disappointed to not have my novel immediately accepted but, if anything, it made me determined that next time I'd get it right. I couldn't waste another eight months writing something that didn't work, so I planned out the new plot meticulously, especially as it was going to be a mystery whodunnit. I wrote my synopsis, then a two-page outline, then a character breakdown for Vicky, Gib, their mum and dad and for the real thieves. The character breakdown was a mini biography for each major character consisting of two to three pages. Only then did I write a chapter breakdown – a paragraph describing what was going to happen in each chapter. It would've been impossible to work out my plot in detail until I felt I really had a handle on my characters because only then would I know how they would react in any given scenario.

Once I was happy that it was all dovetailing together with no holes, I started writing the story, which was completely different to the original one. It took another eight months to complete but I felt the story worked much better and was much tighter. I sent it off again, and this time they said, 'YES!' *Hacker* went on to win the WH Smith Mind-Boggling Book Award and the Young Telegraph / Gimme 5 Children's Book of the Year Award. *Hacker* was my fifth book but my first novel. Eyes on the prize – and the prize for me was proving to myself that I could write a novel. Writing *Hacker* – twice! – taught me a lot, not least about persistence.

38

My next novel, *Operation Gadgetman*, was such fun to write. I really let my imagination run riot with that book. I wanted it to be an entertaining, funny, wacky read. Annie at Transworld accepted it for publication, and I breathed a sigh of relief. Each new book funded a few more months of writing exclusively.

But another year was drawing to a close and I hadn't made much money, barely over a thousand pounds. Just when I began to think I might have to find at least a part-time job to help pay our bills, a production company got in touch with my agent to say they wanted to buy the film rights for *Operation Gadgetman*, and the sum they offered would finance another year of writing.

Yes! I snatched their hand off. I was reprieved.

Was this how publishing worked? TV and film companies would buy dramatisation rights to supplement the incomes of writers? If so, then yes please! I really thought that was all there was to it. Ha! I got busy writing my next novel, *Thief!*, and waited for the first ever dramatisation of one of my stories to be released. When I was sent an advance video of *Gadgetman* – as they had renamed it – Neil and I sat down to watch, both of us beyond excited. I couldn't wait! Ninety minutes later, while the credits were rolling, I turned to Neil and said, 'What the hell?' I had naively assumed that they would keep the main characters as I had written them in my book, i.e. two Black girls and a white girl. But no. In the film, my protagonists had been cast as three white boys. There was only one person of colour in the entire film, in a minor part.

'That's never going to happen again,' I said.

Neil didn't need to ask me what I was talking about.

After what happened with *Operation Gadgetman*, I determined that the next time (if there was a next time) a production company got in touch with me to enquire about buying the rights for one of my books, I wanted to be the one to write the script. But I didn't have a clue how to go about that.

It was time to learn.

I researched script-writing courses and found that the one with the best reputation was run by the National Film and Television School (NFTS) in Beaconsfield, Buckinghamshire. The course was full-time for a month, and the more I read about it, the more I wanted to do it. I wrote my covering letter, enclosed a pristine version of *Not So Stupid!* and sent it off with everything crossed.

A couple of weeks later, NFTS invited me for an interview.

Yes! I'd passed the application-form stage.

Full of self-doubt, I wondered if I would make it any further. I knew nothing, less than nothing, about writing scripts. However, wasn't that what the course was supposed to teach me? I still wasn't making any kind of guaranteed, reasonable living so could I even afford it? Travelling every day from south London to Beaconsfield, a trip of around seventy miles, would not be cheap.

First things first. Time to do some proper research. I headed for my nearest large bookshop and bought all the film scripts I could afford. I headed to my local library and borrowed a lot more. I read them all carefully, making notes where appropriate. No way was I going to rock up at my interview looking like a total noob who couldn't even be bothered to read one script before or after applying for the course.

The day of the interview arrived. I took an early train to

ensure I got there in plenty of time. Plus, I wanted to take a good look at Beaconsfield. As I walked from the station to the school, I couldn't help but admire my surroundings. Beaconsfield had a village feel to it. There was an Oxfam shop on the high street that had last season's designer fashions displayed in the window. Beaconsfield wasn't broke! I finally arrived at the school, amazed at what I saw. It was bigger and more imposing than I'd expected. I wanted in! The butterflies in my stomach began to awaken and flutter. When I care about something, the butterflies always flutter.

I walked into my interview to be confronted by three people, two men and one woman. Sitting in the indicated seat before them, I gave them my sunniest smile, swallowed hard and waited for the first question. After the preliminaries and platitudes had been dispensed with, one of the questions I was asked was, 'What kind of films do you like to watch?'

The moment of truth – or was it? Should I hit them with some art house films I'd watched? Is that what they wanted? Or should I tell the truth about the films I really enjoyed? Bollocks to it! I was going to tell the truth.

'Well, I enjoyed *Terminator, RoboCop, Alien* – after the first thirty minutes, *It's a Wonderful Life, Jason and the Argonauts, Doctor Who and the Daleks* – I prefer the one with Peter Cushing and Bernard Cribbins – and *One Flew Over the Cuckoo's Nest*.'

A look was exchanged between the interviewers. Shit! Had I blown this by being honest?

'Could you tell us why?'

So I took each film in turn and talked about what made them appealing to me, trying not to waffle or witter but to keep my answers succinct and on point.

'I also really enjoyed *Babette's Feast, Jean de Florette* and its sequel *Manon des Sources* and *La Cage aux Folles*,' I added, not wanting them to think I was a total philistine. 'Oh and *The Seventh Seal* with Max von Sydow. I loved that film!' And I enthusiastically told them how and why I considered *The Seventh Seal* a masterpiece and discussed the exciting twists and unexpected, heart-wrenching turns in *Jean de Florette* and *Babette's Feast*. I wasn't lying about those films either. They are all amazing. They asked me questions about some of the other films I'd seen recently. I leaned forward to explain why I liked some and was not so keen on others.

But when I came out of the interview, I was despondent. I hadn't mentioned *mise en scène* or other filmic buzzwords once! The secretary outside the room asked, 'How did it go?'

I shook my head. 'Not too well. I don't think I gave them the answers they were looking for.'

'You should have more faith in yourself,' she told me with a smile.

That was the trouble, I didn't have much faith in myself. Whenever I became excited or angry or passionate about something, I tended to become strident and in-your-face and overly didactic about it. I had tried to soften it over the years and it wasn't as bad as it had been when I was a teen but my enthusiasm could still run away with me.

As I walked home, the spring in my step had turned to concrete blocks in my shoes. *Terminator? RoboCop?* Why on earth had I spoken about them? This was a film school. I should've gone straight for the European films rather than the Hollywood blockbusters. I'd blown it! Once I got home, I moped for the rest of the day, then told myself that there was always next year. I'd just have to try again – and again – until I got in. The following week, I received a letter from the NFTS saying I'd been accepted on their month-long course. Yes!

The trek to Beaconsfield every day for a month was more

than worth it. The atmosphere at the NFTS was wonderful. The students and staff were so welcoming, and the facilities and resources were like none I'd ever experienced before. We analysed films and film scripts in depth, discussing what worked and what didn't, what seemed to work well on paper but then didn't translate onto film and vice versa. I loved every moment. I remember one particularly heated debate about the film *Thelma and Louise*, written by Callie Khouri and directed by Ridley Scott. One of the course tutors and I got into it about the film's ending. My argument was that Thelma and Louise had made a difference to and changed the lives of all the people they'd encountered on their journey towards the end of the film. The tutor's point of view was that the ending sent out a message that if you're a woman who stands up for herself, then it will only end one way – and what kind of message was that? I could see her side, I believe she could see mine. We concluded our heated debate with a smile and a handshake. It was glorious, just the way differences of opinion should be explored and handled – without rancour or negativity. Definitely a life lesson. With each passing day, I felt my knowledge and confidence grow. I really felt that maybe I too could write film scripts.

With one week left, our tutor Jan Fleischer announced that we could apply for a place on the MA Screenwriting course, which would run full-time for eighteen months. If we applied, we would be selected on the basis of our work to date, plus one final project. There was just one problem: there were only six places and at least twelve of us wanted to apply. Eager to be accepted on the MA course, I checked out the full details and my heart sank. There was no way I could afford it and I told Jan so. Jan encouraged me to apply for a bursary should I be accepted onto the course.

I applied and was accepted as one of the six. I also received my bursary, which was a lifeline. The train fares from south London to Beaconsfield were no joke. The NFTS became my home away from home for the next eighteen months.

One exercise we writers had to do was direct a scene from our own graduation scripts. I had never directed in my life and had no clue how to go about it. A professional director was on hand to help us with the process and we had the chance to cast proper actors through Spotlight – an organisation that holds details of theatre, TV and film performers for use by casting directors, directors and producers. I was bricking it! I selected an appropriate scene, which was to take place in a bathroom. I tried to make it sound like I had a handle on everything: every role, every line the actress had to speak, the sound, the lighting – the lot! The director of photography consulted me about the kind of lighting quality I desired for the shot. The sound recordist spoke to me about the quality of the sound I wished to achieve as the actress washed her hands in the scene. I listened to their suggestions, chipped in with the odd comment and thanked them for their input, all the while thinking, 'Can we not just place the camera and set up the lights so I can see what she's doing and just stick the boom mic somewhere where it won't be shot!'

And as for the poor actress – even thinking about it now makes my face burn. She was and is a superb actress, an incredible talent as her many stage, film and TV roles can attest. After a couple of takes where I wasn't quite getting what I wanted – mainly because I hadn't properly spoken to her about what I wanted – I committed a cardinal sin. Instead of discussing her character's emotions and motivations in the scene so she could get a handle on what I was trying to achieve, I tried to tell her how to say a particular line the way I wanted it. Oh, the shame of it! I'm wincing now as I write this. The tutor director just shook his head at me, and I thought, 'Well, I don't know!'

So we tried again. The actress, bless her, delivered what I wanted but she couldn't help being pissed with me and I don't blame her for a single second. Once we had all the raw footage, I then had a week to put it together in one of the editing suites. Now, that bit I loved. Some of my colleagues on the course were natural hyphenates: 'writer-director', 'writer-producer'. If I was ever going to be a hyphenate, it would be 'writer-editor', which isn't really a thing, but I loved the process of putting a narrative together using hardware and software. In fact, I loved editing so much that I promised myself if my writing career fizzled out, I would actively pursue editing.

One thing was for sure: I was no director and resolved to leave that role to others. I sucked at it. But it didn't matter because the experience was positive in that it gave me an insight into how words on a page get translated into footage on the screen and the roles of all those involved in making that happen. It also gave me an insight into just how much a particular vision can change between a script and what the director imagines, and how the story may be changed via the editing process.

Our tutor Jan Fleischer had been on my interview panel and, when I'd been at the school for a few months, I asked him, 'What made you pick me for the month-long course? Because I really thought I'd blown it with the selection of films I told you that I liked.'

Jan smiled. 'Lorie, you have an incredibly strong sense of story and a real understanding of what makes a narrative work or not. We can help students to improve their techniques but there must be something there to build on, and you have that.'

I did? His words made me start with surprise. Creating stories was like breathing to me. I couldn't imagine not doing so, which meant I thought everyone could do the same. Was the art of telling stories down to nature or nurture? I felt sure that reading for pleasure from early childhood had nurtured the passion in me to create my own stories. I believe the craft and business of writing can be taught, and the art of writing can be honed, as a part of it means trusting in your own voice to tell a story – and all of these require tenacity and perseverance.

Jan's secretary had been right, I should've had more faith in myself – but it was so hard. My parents and my mum in particular had always encouraged me to stand up for myself when necessary, but sometimes it felt like the world was telling me to make myself as small and as silent as possible to fit in. Not only did I suffer badly from imposter syndrome, but it took a while to trust in my own style and voice in the telling of my stories. Ironically, I later realised that the thing I thought was holding me back – using my real, authentic voice and style when telling stories – was the very thing that was moving me forward. I have met so many people who also suffer from imposter syndrome and it's a trap that slows you down or stops you in your tracks. My remedy when I realised just how much it was holding me back was to acknowledge its presence, then to actively try to ignore it.

I'm not going to lie; even now that's still a work in progress. I still tend to think 'why me?' when I get invited to swanky places, or I surreptitiously pinch myself when I meet famous people that I admire. If I get emails or correspondence inviting me to take part in something I could previously only ever dream of, I tend to check the name of the recipient – and more than once – somehow convinced that the invitation has been sent to the wrong person. Like I said, a work in progress.

I will always be grateful to the NFTS for the help, support, encouragement and education they provided. I learned so much and had a chance to explore other skills, like directing, at which

I was useless, and editing, which I loved. It also helped with the writing of my books because after I'd finished my course, I couldn't help but write each story as if it was a film playing inside my head, with me desperately trying to describe the scene, the setting, the plot, the characters and their dialogue as well as their emotions and motivations. The course honed my plotting skills and taught me to trust my instincts. The NFTS opened doors for me. It was now up to me to walk through them.

39

One of the scariest film scenes I remember seeing as a child is from *7 Faces of Dr Lao* – a peculiar fantasy film containing a magic circus and a huge monster. That's probably why I enjoyed it. I was all about fantasy films; *Dr Who*, *Sinbad* films, *Village of the Damned*, *Children of the Damned* and *Jason and the Argonauts* were all favourites. *Dr Lao* starred Tony Randall, who played seven different parts including the titular main character, a Chinese circus owner. His performance as a Chinese man was almost as cringeworthy as Mickey Rooney's depiction of Mr Yunioshi, supposedly a Japanese man, in the film *Breakfast at Tiffany's*. However, there was a scene in *Dr Lao* that was brutal in its honesty and it jolted me like a hard slap when I first watched it. I had occasion to watch the film again in my early twenties, and the same scene hit harder still and dug deeper. In my twenties, it was painful to watch and I'm sure it played a part in the decision-making and life choices I made since then.

In the scene, a vain, silly, middle-aged woman, Mrs Cassin, consults Apollonius of Tyana, a fortune teller at Dr Lao's circus who is cursed with telling the truth whether his clients want to hear it or not. Mrs Cassin wants to know when she will find oil on her land and when she will be married again.

Apollonius tells her, 'When you die, you will be buried and forgotten. And that is all. And for all the good or evil, creation or destruction your living might have accomplished, you might just as well never have lived at all.'

I don't pretend to have all the answers, or indeed any of them, but it seemed to me at the time – and now – that surely we are put on this earth to leave it a better place than when we joined it? Otherwise, what's the point?

In my twenties, when I watched the film again, it struck me that I didn't want to end up like Mrs Cassin. Deep down, I believed the doctor I'd overheard at Huddersfield Infirmary was probably correct and I wouldn't live much past thirty. I didn't want to live and die having never made a positive difference to somebody, somewhere, at some time. That would be such a waste. But I made the mistake of thinking that leaving the world a better place meant becoming a famous movie or pop star and entertaining millions, or becoming a scientist, engineer or inventor and saving the world in some manner, shape or form. It was only as I grew older and hopefully wiser that I realised my thinking had left the goal of improving the world attainable to only a select few. I discovered that there are many ways to change the world or save a life.

A friendly smile
A spontaneous chat
A helping hand
A hand to hold
An offer of a sandwich and a cup of tea
An understanding nod
A kind word.

A friendly smile
A listening ear
A cheery wave
A sympathetic hand on someone's shoulder
A hug

A lone voice
A conversation.

A friendly smile.
Standing up to be counted,
Sitting down to show solidarity
A vote
A handshake
A noisy protest
A silent tear
And did I mention, a friendly smile.

That's how you make a difference.
Just sayin'.

Representation

40

The first thing any aspiring writer needs to realise, and which took me longer than it should've to grasp, is that publishing is a business. It's not a charity, it's not an altruistic enterprise, it's a business. And if a publishing house fails to make money, they go under. It's as simple and complex as that. When I first started out as an author, I thought that the children's market would be different from the computing world in that there would be less bias, less prejudice, less bullshit to put up with. Ha! When I started meeting editors from various publishing houses, it dawned on me that all I'd done was swap one set of high-heeled, pinch-toe shoes for another. That's not to say that all editors were the same or treated me the same. Hell no. Some of my editors have been an absolute joy to work with and I would've got nowhere without their help, support and backing. But there were others who weren't so pleasant.

I remember one editor employed by one of the top ten UK publishers who, when offered a second book, told me bluntly, 'Oh no, Malorie. We only wanted a book from you for our multicultural list. We don't need another.'

Message received and understood.

I never worked with that editor or for that publisher again.

Early in my career, I was invited to a meeting with two editors to discuss a story of mine that they said they would like to publish. I rocked up and saw the surprise on their faces when they noted that I was Black. I was led to the senior editor's office and, after the pleasantries had been exchanged, we got onto the topic of illustrations. The senior editor asked, 'So, Malorie, how do you see your characters?'

'Black,' I replied at once.

The two women before me exchanged a look. I knew where this was going.

'Well, would you mind if we made your family white instead of Black?' asked the senior editor.

'Why?' I asked.

'Well, we already have a book that features a Black family,' came the reply.

'How many books do you have that feature white families?' I asked.

Silence.

'Well, would you mind if we made them Asian then?' asked the younger editor.

My knowledge of Asian and East Asian culture was embarrassingly limited. I asked, 'What kind of Asian ethnicity are you thinking of? Indian? Pakistani? Chinese? Japanese? Malaysian?'

Silence.

Ah well! That's the end of getting my book published by these people, I thought as the conversation moved on to less loaded subjects like possible illustrators and publication dates. I walked out of the meeting with a view to phoning my agent as soon as I got home to ask him to start sending out my story text again to other publishers. The pointed silences between my answers to their questions had spoken volumes. But, to my surprise, I received a letter two days later, informing me that the senior editor had decided that they would be doing me a 'disservice' in asking me to change the ethnicities of my characters. I was grateful because it was an excellent list and I was proud to be on it. Plus, working with the senior and junior editors taught me a lot about writing first chapter books in terms of the layout, the marriage between text and illustrations, the use of appropriate vocabulary and the structuring of stories for that particular age range.

Do I resent them asking me to make my characters white? Resent is the wrong word. Did it surprise me that they asked? Yes, it did, but I like to think that our conversation was instructive on both sides. I know that after their letter stating that they would publish me after all, we had a perfectly amicable working relationship. And I don't doubt for a second that taking on my book required some fierce arguing from the commissioning editor at their next internal acquisitions meeting. I worked with the senior and junior editors on more books after that. They took a number of my suggestions on board, though not my request to ask the illustrator to provide more variety of expression and visage in the illustrations for my books, but you can't win them all.

Illustrations in children's books are a thorny topic. A major part of the issue is that a number of white illustrators don't seem to be able to draw Black people with any degree of accuracy, variety or sensitivity. Drawing people from various ethnicities appears to be absent from the curriculum of too many art schools. Some illustrators would draw white faces then add cross-hatching to denote a person of colour. Some would draw the same black face and just make it bigger or smaller to differentiate the children from adults and would change the hairstyle to differentiate between male and female. And some drew caricatures that would've found a welcome home in less enlightened periods of history where literature exaggerated Black people's features for comedic effect and as so-called 'proof' of our supposed inferiority. Trying to find a way to let various editors know that, as far as I was concerned, certain illustrators

they had in mind for my books were non-starters required dip-
lomatic reserves I didn't know I had. Sometimes I lost the argument; more often I won. But once again, I felt I had to use my
voice to express my concerns because I knew some editors had
never before considered the objections I made. They couldn't
see what was glaringly obvious to me until after it was pointed
out.

The illustrator who worked on most of the first editions of
my books for Transworld was Derek Brazell and his artwork
was – and is – phenomenal. A major part of the appeal of a
book for any child or teenager is the image on the jacket. I feel
incredibly fortunate that Derek was the one to illustrate the original jackets on my novels such as *Hacker*, *Operation Gadgetman*,
Thief!, *Pig-Heart Boy* and *Dangerous Reality*.

I've also been extremely lucky to work with Dapo Adeola,
illustrator extraordinaire on our book *We're Going to Find the
Monster*. I really enjoy the work of illustrators who not only
translate the text they are given but add to it with their own
vision. The talented John Aggs, who illustrated the graphic
novel of *Noughts and Crosses* (adapted so skilfully by Ian Edgin-
ton), is another artist who brought more to the story via their
artwork. Illustrators can make or break a picture book or
indeed any book with illustrations, so the correct choice is
vital.

I once attended an event where the speaker (I can't remember who it was, but I remember what they said!) was talking
about book jackets. She said that if the buying public doesn't
recognise an author's name, the book jacket is a two-second
advertisement before their eyes move on to the next title. If you
manage to grab them with the book cover and you're lucky, the
potential buyer might pick it up and read the blurb on the back.
And if you're very, very lucky, they might read the first page.

That's how long you have – and the tools you have – to grab them. I've never forgotten that and it's why I will try to state my case clearly if I feel a book jacket or the blurb on the back isn't working as it should.

Employing your voice isn't just about using it when telling stories, it's about using it to produce those stories as well. This doesn't mean that you don't listen to advice from those who may have more experience in their field of publishing than you do, but it doesn't hurt to have a clear vision and the reasoning to back that up. But remember, listening to advice and being flexible doesn't hurt either. If there's one thing I've learned in over thirty years in publishing, it's that you have to know what battle to pick and when to pick it.

Onwards and upwards.

I was once invited for lunch by a production company who were interested in buying the film rights to *Noughts and Crosses*. A very fancy restaurant in the West End of London was booked and three people from the company – a creative director and two producers – were already at the table by the time I arrived, which was precisely on time. Warm greetings and amiable small talk were exchanged while we all perused the extensive, expensive menu. Food ordered, we got down to business. The creative director of the production company waxed lyrical about my book, the depth and breadth and height of his love for the story and how he thought it could work as a film. They had a couple of scriptwriters in mind who would be perfect for the project and had some ideas for changes that they hoped I'd be amenable to.

'What kind of changes are you thinking of?' I asked.

A look was exchanged between the production company employees.

'How would you feel about making the Crosses Asian rather than Black?' came the question.

Say what? Not this again!

'When you say Asian, what d'you mean?' I asked.

'Er . . . well, we haven't quite nailed that down yet but we were thinking maybe Indian or perhaps East Asian?'

What did that mean? Chinese? Japanese? Korean? Mongolian? What?

'I see,' I said. 'May I ask why?'

'We just feel we would reach a bigger audience that way,' said the creative director.

'Hmm. Not with my book you're not,' I thought.

The creative director and producers continued to talk about how the film might work. I sat and ate the delicious courses and nodded at the appropriate moments as if I was listening hard, all the while thinking, 'I became an author because of the shortage of Black protagonists in books. There's still a scarcity of Black main characters in films and TV unless they have a gun in their hand, and now you want to take my work that features a Black protagonist and render us invisible again? Hell no, squared.'

Still, it was an excellent lunch. The crème brûlée was on point.

Just sayin'.

41

I believe that anything a child or teen can experience or has to live through is a legitimate subject to write about. It's all in the way it is handled. Sensitive subjects shouldn't be shied away from – that tells a child or teen that what they have gone through or are currently going through should be buried, rather than spoken or written about. It reinforces the erroneous notion that the child or young adult is alone. Speaking from experience, that's so damaging. So even though I have been and will continue to be criticised for the subject matter in a few of my books, will that stop me?

No, it won't! Guaranteed.

Part of my job as a fiction writer is to give a voice to those who perhaps don't have one yet – and also to tell the truth. Stories have to contain that element of truth to be believable. No matter how fanciful the plot or setting, readers need to believe in the characters' motivations and actions. These need to call to something inside the reader that they recognise and can relate to. Emotions are universal, and we all share or have the ability to empathise as well as sympathise with the feelings of others if this is nurtured and encouraged from an early age.

I tell myself to beware of those who will hate you for making them feel uncomfortable. That's not the word they will use, but they will come for you if you make them feel bad, mostly about themselves. The latest war against representation stems from a movement against certain books with predominantly

Black or gay characters, or subject matter that questions race or sexuality in society and history.

I personally have been accused of 'race-baiting' whenever I say something critical of a white person. Race-baiting. I ask you! It's such BS. It's also a short but sharp lesson.

In the broken-mirror times we live in, telling the truth about history, about how Western countries acquired and accumulated their wealth, i.e. from centuries of slavery, is now called 'critical race theory' and is banned in some quarters. Critical race theory is an old term and concept whose core idea is that race is a social rather than biological construct and that racism is not merely a product of the prejudices and biases of individuals but is embedded in societal systems and policies. However, in recent years its meaning has been twisted and it's given as an example of a concept that sows division within schools. Genuine critical race theory involves the teaching of the truth – the truth about slavery, about how Black people were and are treated due to racism. Take the word 'woke' – a term widely used since the 1930s in African American activism and in popular culture to mean someone who has become conscious of and alert to social injustice experienced as a Black person. This term has been co-opted negatively and subverted by white mainstream media and the right wing as a cheap retort when confronted with their own bigotry.

Can't make racist jokes any more without being challenged?

'Oh, the "woke" are out to get me.'

Can't make racist statements any more without being called out about it?

'Wokeness is stifling free speech and debate.'

Give me a massive break!

History has become a school fruit-salad exercise. Some governments or authorities in the West are demanding that teachers pick out the 'good bits', the flattering parts of history, and discard the rest. That shouldn't be the way it works. If I could go back in time and give myself as a teen three pieces of advice, one of them would be to seek out and learn the truth – and for the love of God don't become one of the sheeple who believe everything they are told and everything they read in the papers because they're too lazy, weary or gullible to search out the truth for themselves.

42

It wasn't just in school where I didn't see positive portrayals of Black people. I grew up watching films and TV programmes where the vast majority of the protagonists were white. As I've already described, all the books I read at school, until I was seventeen and studied *Othello*, featured white protagonists. Shared stories – whether they are texts that are studied by a whole class, stories that teachers read to their students, or stories that are passed around and recommended by word of mouth – are one of the best ways to engender and nurture empathy. I believed, particularly after the Stephen Lawrence case, that there had to be a way of enabling white people to walk in our shoes for a while. To experience what it was like to suffer erasure or discrimination – a cliché word for something that is so every day, ongoing, pervasive and incredibly painful.

The books I read presented me with alternatives ways of thinking, of doing, of being. They also showed me what I was missing, and crucially that *I* was missing. Stories have the power to inspire and ignite imaginations. Through reading I believed that if I worked long enough and hard enough, then maybe I too could find the key to opening life's locked doors, which would lead not only to knowledge and understanding, but to opportunity. I had to believe that – or what would be the point?

That's why representation was and is so important. Not just important, but vital. If I had never read any books by Black authors, would it have occurred to me that I too could become one? I seriously doubt it. A love of reading made me want to write my own stories and poems from a young age, but it was reading novels by Black authors when I was in my twenties that made me consider writing as a career.

I know of so many other authors from underrepresented backgrounds – LGBTQ+, physically and mentally challenged, neurodivergent, Traveller and Romany heritage, working class – who say the same thing. It's hard to be it when you don't see it. There is more than enough room in all creative spheres for myriad voices from varied backgrounds. This adds to the quality, richness and diversity of the stories we get to experience.

D'you want to know one of the best aspects of my job? When younger authors tell me that my books played a part in either making them readers or making them writers – or both. To hear that is so humbling and gratifying. No child, whatever their background, should feel invisible in the world of literature.

As a child, I genuinely thought racism wouldn't exist by the time I was middle-aged. Ha! Yes, OK, I thought and spoke and hoped as a child. But was the thought so outlandish? I didn't think so. The optimism of youth. But, you know what? Part of me still hopes that one day, someday, that will be the case. It won't happen in my lifetime – but surely one day a change must come?

43

In the early 1990s, as I approached the end of my second year as a full-time writer, a publishing house got in touch to ask if I'd be prepared to write a book for them. The book would be part of a series of stories featuring the same characters and written by a number of different authors. At that time, the advance was phenomenal – five thousand pounds, almost double what I was earning for a single book advance. However, there was a catch.

My name wouldn't be on the jacket and the company wanted me to sign away all my moral rights to the story. I'd have to give up my copyright. That meant that if the book was dramatised in any way, serialised, or exploited in any manner, shape or form, I wouldn't receive another penny. That was why the advance was so generous. I had to think long and hard about it. God knows the money would've been very welcome to help finance another several months of writing, but one of the first pieces of advice I'd received in my very first writing group at the City Lit was *never* give up your copyright. Giving up my copyright felt like not just giving up my voice but giving it to someone else. I had worked too hard for years and received too many rejection letters not to see my name on the book jacket. It wasn't vanity per se; it was a desire not to revert back to invisibility.

I took a deep breath, called myself all kinds of fool, and said no.

And watched as the series sold incredibly well, but without my input.

I confess, I don't regret it. All power to the authors who did write for the series. It was a great way to make money and experience writing to someone else's brief, which is a really useful skill to have. I did a similar thing when I wrote for the CBBC series *Byker Grove* for a few years in the early 2000s, and also when, in 2017, I co-wrote with Chris Chibnall *Rosa*, an episode of *Doctor Who* where the Doctor meets a heroine of mine – and hers! – Rosa Parks.

44

Most, if not all, authors and illustrators wish for their work to be dramatised in some manner. I've been blessed enough to have had some of my books turned into TV dramas and theatre productions. To date *Noughts and Crosses* has been two different theatre plays – adapted by Dominic Cooke for the RSC in 2008 and Sabrina Mahfouz for Pilot Theatre in 2019. It has also been a two-series TV drama made by Mammoth Productions for the BBC.

I'm not going to lie. It is so strange to see real-life actors become the characters that you've created from your own imagination. The characters who have only existed in your head are suddenly all right there in front of you. Yes, it is actors inhabiting a role, but to hear them say your words or to see them living the life that you created for them, well, that 'wow' feeling never gets old!

In dramatisations, when my characters are going through tough times, I feel it as well as see it. When they're indulging in sexy times, my face blazes hot. When they're going through miserable times, I want to cry with them. I suffer from acute second-hand embarrassment and the emotions of others are often adopted as if they were my own. Which is very useful when it comes to writing my characters, but when watching dramatisations or just living life it's a pain in the arse. I was once described by a friend as being too empathetic for my own good. I'm not a fan of hearts that bleed all over the place, including my own. Sometimes I have to tell myself sternly to get a grip.

But I will never get tired, jaded or blasé about seeing my characters brought to life on stage or screen.

As an author, you have to be aware that the dramatisation is *never* going to be exactly the same as the book, nor should it be. What works on the page might not work on screen and vice versa. Besides, the cover versions of songs that I much prefer are the ones which don't sound the same as the original. If you're going to duplicate rather than innovate, what's the point?

If you're an author who hates to have your work chopped and changed, don't sell the dramatisation rights. Part of the process of selling such rights is to trust you have placed your work in good hands and then let it go. I feel incredibly lucky that most of my dramatisation experiences have been positive and have taught me a lot. I appreciate that not every author or illustrator can say the same.

It has been fascinating to watch the reaction to the BBC / Mammoth Studios production of *Noughts and Crosses* on the TV. Some adults have had their noses well and truly put out of joint at the thought of a Britain where Black people are the majority and/or hold most of the positions of power. To the extent that they have followed the book around the internet, trashing it whenever they can. I even had a woman ask me to contact her daughter's school to get them to withdraw my book from study as she – the mum – felt the subject matter was not suitable for teens. She wanted me to explain that *Noughts and Crosses* should only be read by adults, even though I originally wrote it for teens-plus. When I declined, she wrote back to me stating that she shouldn't have expected anything else. She seriously wanted me to contact her daughter's school (the mother admitted that it was her, not her daughter, who had a problem with the book) and ask them to withdraw all copies of my book from the school library and classrooms and to ask them to stop teaching it because she was uncomfortable with the subject matter.

Yeah, right.

Most of the books I've written for teens have been criticised by adults regarding their suitability. No teen has ever contacted me or told me that they thought the subject matter of my books was too much for teens to handle. Ever.

If my books and any resulting dramatisations make some adults nervous or uncomfortable then maybe I'm doing my job right.

45

I am not a role model. Please don't call me one. I'm not a role model, nor do I want to be one. But when I was Children's Laureate I was very aware that as the UK's first Black Children's Laureate, my actions would not only be considered a reflection of me and my character, but of how well any Black person in the role would perform. Isn't it funny-peculiar how every person of colour finds themselves representing everyone else of colour? Jeez, I hate that phrase – person of colour! It's one of those phrases like BAME – Black, Asian and minority ethnic. It's supposed to mean anyone who isn't white. Everyone else is lumped into one disparate mass. 'Everyone else' is not a homogenous grouping.

We 'people of colour', especially Black people, need to stop seeing ourselves and judging ourselves via the gaze of white people. White people are not the global standard. Their hair, their bodies, their way of thinking is not the standard by which everyone else on the planet should be assessed and judged. We seriously need to move away from that kind of thinking. As Bob Marley sang, it is a form of mental slavery and we need to break free from its shackles.

I remember having an argument with a white person back in the day about Jamaican patois. I argued that patois isn't bad English, it's a language in and of itself with strong roots in English but it has its own syntax and etymology. They kept telling me that I was wrong. It took me back to all the times my dad used to rebuke me for not speaking 'the Queen's English'. I understand now that he had internalised that the way he expressed himself, the way he spoke, even his accent, were less than.

If you're a Scottish, Welsh or Geordie writer, using your own authentic idioms and phrases in your writing is perfectly valid. No one would dispute that. Whatever region you come from, adding regional phrases and ways of thinking and being contribute authenticity and texture to dialogue, thoughts and action. Surely it's this specificity that makes stories universal? It allows readers to see that even though characters may be born or live in regions far from or different to their own, we can still share the same desires, concerns, joys, passions and sorrows. And characters may act in a way that perhaps the reader may not, but it's up to the writer to make their views and actions plausible. As readers we don't have to agree with a character's actions but we should understand why they have acted in a certain way.

I once had a conversation about one of my books in which I was asked what the theme of my story was. I answered, only to be told by the two white people I was speaking to that I'd got it wrong, and the theme was something entirely different. They weren't arguing about what I might have been thinking subconsciously when I wrote it, which would've been an interesting conversation. No, they were telling me that the theme wasn't what I thought it was. Now if you get less, more or something entirely different in the reading of one of my stories to what I had in mind when I wrote it, then all power to you and your elbow. Isn't that the way reading works? Each person's life experiences inevitably colour the way they interpret what they are reading. That's what makes story discussions so fascinating. But when I tell you what I had in mind when I wrote a story or poem, please don't tell me that I'm wrong and I had something else in mind entirely. That form of gaslighting is also called denying my voice.

Just sayin'.

Love

46

During my first full-time job at a software house, there was one man in particular on the project who was lovely to me. A six-feet-tall Scottish guy called Neil. Every time we were in the terminal room together – a room filled with PCs where everyone congregated to get their computing work done – he'd be the first to come over to me if I got stuck or had a query. He was an outrageous flirt – strictly banter, no wandering hands. Every time he went out to buy lunch, he'd make a point of asking if he could get me anything. If I said no because I wanted something in the opposite direction to the way he was going, he'd insist on getting it for me anyway.

After one such conversation, Neil headed off to get my lunch and my colleague Paul turned to me and said, 'You can wrap that man around your little finger.'

I laughed it off because, I mean, come on. Of course I couldn't. Neil was just a nice guy. He'd do the same for everyone, I thought. Back in the day Neil had been his university's karate champion. He also used to play rugby and was built like a brick outhouse. The thing I *really* liked about him was he could always make me laugh. He had a wicked sense of humour. I've always been drawn to men who can make me laugh. It wasn't long before I counted Neil as a friend, a true friend. But that was all he was. Or so I thought . . .

It was 14 May 1981 and Neil and I were in the terminal room, working late. We were making small talk and Neil was telling bad jokes. So far, so familiar. He kept smiling at me. And it didn't click. He asked if I needed any help. And it didn't click. After thirty minutes or so, I said, 'Neil, how do you do this? I'm stuck!' He came over, eager as a faithful Labrador.

'Wow! He likes solving puzzles,' I thought.

'You don't have to come over,' I said, not wanting to interrupt his work any more than I had to. 'Just tell me how to do this.'

'Let the dog see the rabbit,' he replied, beckoning for me to get up, so he could sit down in front of my monitor.

'Can't you just tell me?' I suggested.

'Better if I see it,' said Neil.

I walked off to pull up a chair, so I could sit next to him.

'You can sit on my lap if you want,' he said.

And *still* it didn't click.

He was a flirty bastard. So no big deal. I sat on his lap to get a better view of what he was doing. A much better view than pulling up a chair would have afforded me. Neil told me what I'd done wrong and how to put it right. He was so sweet, so patient. I thanked him and went to stand up. And then he looked at me – and I looked at him. His face moved slowly towards mine, allowing me time to move away if I wanted. And I thought, 'Is this man going to kiss me? He's not going to kiss me, is he?'

And then he was. Kissing me. On the lips.

And I thought, 'This guy is kissing me!'

I didn't even know he liked me that way. There we were, liplocking up a storm until a colleague walked into the terminal room and caught us. We sprung apart like guilty thieves caught stealing kisses. Oh, the shame! Oh, the embarrassment! Cheeks burning, face on fire, I fled. It was definitely time to go home. Neil caught up with me as I was putting my coat on and heading for the lift.

'That guy has bad timing.' Neil tried to make a joke out of it.

'Maybe it's just as well,' I replied.

Neil nodded and asked, 'Would you like to have dinner with me sometime this week?'

So he wasn't just trying it on? He really did like me?

'OK,' I replied evenly, though my heart was thumping.

I realised that once again I'd done things arse about face. The dating should've come before the kissing. But if the man hadn't kissed me I would never have picked up on all the hints he'd been dropping for months. It only clicked when he kissed me. Sometimes I'm so slow on the uptake, I confound even myself.

For example, in the first *Shrek* film, when Donkey is being thrown up into the air while Fiona is going through the wedding ceremony with Lord Farquaad, Donkey tells Shrek that they have to wait for the priest to ask if anyone has any objections to the marriage. Donkey watches for this moment, only to realise they've left it too late and he exclaims, 'Mother Fletcher! He's already said it.'

'Who was Mother Fletcher?' I wondered when watching the film. A previous owner of Donkey? Someone from his past he was recalling that we, the audience, had yet to meet?

I only realised what he was really saying when I watched it for the second time on TV!

Mother Fletcher, but I'm slow!

Neil and I went to dinner one night, and then the cinema another, and after a while we started dating seriously, exclusively. Forty-one years later, we're still together. Every anniversary of that day in the terminal room (14 May – also our wedding anniversary), I tell him, 'My tolerance is astounding.'

Every anniversary, he replies, 'My patience is amazing.'

And we're both right.

47

In 2012, I received an unexpected email asking if I would be interested in being shortlisted for the role of the next Children's Laureate. The role was initially devised in the late 1990s by the then-Poet Laureate Ted Hughes and children's author Michael Morpurgo. The very first Children's Laureate was Quentin Blake. The two-year role involves being an advocate for all things related to children's reading, literature and literacy. The beauty of the role is that each laureate can make it their own. Michael Rosen established a teachers' resource programme – Poetry Friendly Classrooms – and set up the Roald Dahl Funny Prize, which ran from 2008 to 2013; Jacqueline Wilson campaigned to have parents read aloud to their children; Anthony Browne worked to get more children drawing; Julia Donaldson developed an anthology called *Poems to Perform* to encourage very young children to have fun with drama performances. Each laureate to date had brought their own interests, skills and personality to the role, so I figured – 'why not?' Plus, my daughter was about to head off for university, which made the timing ideal. I threw my hat into the ring and thought nothing more of it. A while later, I received another email offering me the position if I wanted it.

And I was surprised by how much I did.

Until it was specifically offered to me, I was flattered to be asked but told myself that it would probably go no further. Now that the role was potentially mine, I thought carefully about what I'd be taking on. I had a meeting with the Children's

Laureate steering committee where we had a full and frank discussion about opportunities and benefits, and where I voiced my concerns about how much writing I'd get done in my two-year tenure. But it was far too good an opportunity to let slip through my fingers. One deep breath and a gulp later, I confirmed that I would be honoured to take on the role and left the meeting feeling like I was about to embark on a great new adventure. I was also terrified! This was way outside my comfort zone. I hated making speeches (still do!) and I didn't much like being in the public eye (still don't!). But that's a major part of the reason I took on the role – to blast myself outside of my comfort zone. When such zones get too comfy they tend to grow almost imperceptibly smaller and smaller, until they can actually restrict your growth. I knew I had to give it a try, otherwise I would regret it for the rest of my life. It felt like a now-or-never moment.

When my tenure was officially announced I was officially the eighth Children's Laureate, following in Julia Donaldson's illustrious footsteps. Where she had predominantly worked with infant school-age children, I decided that my remit would be to try and encourage secondary school-age children to read more. The brief I set myself was simple – more children and young adults, reading more.

In my two years in the role I travelled up and down the UK visiting schools in Scotland, Wales, England and Northern Ireland. And I *loved* it. Meeting young adults, chatting to them about what interests them, what concerns them, what moves them and then trying to recommend books accordingly was the highlight of my tenure. And being Children's Laureate opened the door to so many opportunities, some of which I grasped with both hands – like the chance to set up the first UK young adult literature convention as part of the

London Film and Comic Convention – and some of which got a hard pass.

I have always and will always count myself fortunate to have had the opportunity to try and switch more teenagers on to the pleasures of reading in all its forms and formats – including graphic novels, narrative verse stories and illustrated books – and to bang the drum for more inclusion regarding the writers, illustrators and protagonists published in the UK. Some parts of the press tried to spin my words to make it seem like my only concern was Black children or that I had some kind of visceral dislike of white children, but all I could do was try to counter such claims as and when they occurred. All too often the mainstream media publish their stories forgetting or not caring that real people and their lives are attached to the other end of what they write.

Being Children's Laureate was an overwhelmingly positive, if exhausting, experience. I thought there would be time and space for me to carry on writing during my tenure, but that didn't happen. I spent the two years reading research papers on education and literacy, writing articles, appearing on radio and TV, visiting schools, and taking part in events and literary festivals – all of which left very little space for anything else.

While I loved being Children's Laureate, I was also afraid of messing up. The press made a lot of the fact that I was the first Black Children's Laureate. I knew if I mucked up, it wouldn't be 'Malorie Blackman stuffs up!' It would be 'Black author and first Black Children's Laureate stuffs up!' Being Black in the UK in a public-facing role means you end up representing – whether you want to or not. I knew if I took on the role, I didn't want to half-arse it. I'd either do it to the best of my ability or I wouldn't do it at all and not waste everyone's time, including my own. That's why I took on more than I had to, said yes to more than

I needed to and tried to make my two years count. The role was a labour of love – where labour balanced equally and sometimes weighed more heavily than the love part!

The haters and detractors during that time – and since – are never going to make me feel sorry that I took on the role. It seems to me that there are those who have a vested interest in trying to ensure that women in general and Black women in particular never use their voices. Look at the abuse women in politics have to put up with, especially Black women like Diane Abbott or Dawn Butler. Indeed, any woman in the public eye is considered fair game by some. That's why my view has always been to try and link arms with others so that we can make sure that when one of us gets knocked down, there are many others to help them get back up again.

The haters won't win. They can't.

48

2010.

In my mid-to-late fifties, though I was still standing – just! – my health nosedived. Sickle cell crises, which I'd only had to endure two or three times a year, became far more frequent, sometimes two or three times a month. My whole life was disrupted. Writing took far longer because around two weeks of every month were spent in bed knocking back painkillers. It got so bad I began to wish that the doctor and nurse who had pronounced at the foot of my bed when I was eighteen had actually been right. Life was growing unbearable.

One really bad crisis had me giving in and agreeing, albeit reluctantly, to go to hospital. It was during that stay that a doctor asked me what regular medication I was taking for my sickle cell. I didn't have a clue what he was talking about.

'I don't take regular medication, I just take pain relief when it gets really bad,' I frowned.

'But we have a couple of treatments we could try to alleviate your symptoms,' he told me. 'Has no one previously explained this to you?'

'No. No one.'

'Have you not been going to your outpatient appointments?'

'I haven't been offered any appointments since I moved house twenty years ago,' I replied.

When I moved house, I moved from one local authority to

another and fell between the cracks as far as my medical notes being passed on was concerned. I could've pursued it, but I didn't, as I'd had enough of hospitals at that point.

'Oh dear! You should've been seen once a year at the absolute minimum,' said the doctor. 'We could've alleviated your symptoms years ago.'

I was stunned.

'You mean, all this time I've been suffering unnecessarily?' I thought.

In all fairness, I had avoided going to hospital so how could any doctor have told me that there were now treatments to be had for my disorder?

'So what treatment could I have?' I asked eagerly.

'Well, your foetal haemoglobin level is really low. In fact, it's what we would see in people with full-blown sickle cell anaemia.'

Well, that explained a lot. No wonder I was having so many crises per month. Foetal haemoglobin didn't sickle. My adult blood cells did so on a regular basis. My disorder had killed off my spleen in my twenties. I knew that slowly but surely it would do the same to the rest of me.

'We could start you on a course of chemotherapy,' said the doctor.

Excuse me? 'A course of *what*?'

'Chemotherapy. We would give you chemo drugs which would destroy your sickling blood and after several months it would be replaced by foetal blood cells, which are much less prone to sickling.'

Chemotherapy? Wouldn't I just be exchanging one set of problems with another? 'And the side effects?' I asked.

A pause. 'Well, there are of course side effects, as what you're taking is a chemo drug. It's called hydroxycarbamide. Others who have taken it have experienced extreme tiredness and of course your immune system would be compromised and your hair may thin or even fall out, but hopefully the long-term gains would outweigh any disadvantages.'

An arrangement was made for a haematology doctor from King's College Hospital to phone me to discuss the option at length when I returned home. And discuss it at length we did and then some. There were so many side effects it wasn't even funny but, quite frankly, I was sick and tired of sickle cell crises rendering me useless for two weeks out of every four, so I said yes. And in 2020, by some strange quirk of fortune, I started the treatment around the same time as the Covid pandemic lockdown began. I was warned that I would be in the extremely vulnerable category for quite some time but during lockdown my trips out of the house would be severely limited anyway, so that was my lockdown silver lining.

I suffered a number of side effects – dizziness, headaches and nausea for the first several weeks, followed in the next several months by hair thinning, alopecia, skin rashes . . . and, oh my goodness, the tiredness. I was tired all the time. Walking up one flight of stairs would leave me breathless. But even with all that, it was still better than having crises.

It seems bizarre that to alleviate my sickle cell symptoms, I need to take a chemo drug every day, but it appears to be working. The drugs massacred my immune system for a long while, so during the pandemic I sometimes felt like I was under house arrest, but God knows there were too many who were far worse off than I was. So many lost loved ones to Covid and couldn't even say a proper goodbye. Watching the news every day certainly put my piddly little issues into perspective.

When I'm counting my blessings – which I try to do every day – I'm grateful for modern medicine and a drug which may be ruining my hair and knackering my immune system but which has also reduced the number and severity of the sickle cell crises I was having to endure.

A fair trade. I'll take that.

49

Hmm . . . OK, let's go there!

If you were to ask me, 'Do you believe in God?' I would take a moment and reply, 'Yes, I think I do, particularly on really good days and really bad days.'

On beautiful spring days, I see God in every tree, in the blue skies, in birdsong and flowers. On cold, crisp winter days, I see her in every flake of snow. I see her in warm smiles and kind gestures. That's my God. I believe in her.

In religion, not so much.

I give a crazy-hard swerve to born-again Christians who spout their racism or homophobia like they think God is whispering directly into their ears. Those who believe their god is instructing them to hate and hurt others don't believe in the same God as I do. The anti-abortionists who believe in the rights of the unborn child but are then content to let that child starve or go without medical care while it lives do my head in.

My God is love. And peace. And live and let live. And laughter. And floating upwards. My God demands that I forgive others who have wronged me. That's a work in slow progress. She demands that I be a pacifist. And I try, God knows I try. I think I was – mostly – until I had my daughter. Then my pacifism dissolved like soluble aspirin.

So how does my faith influence my writing?

Because alongside love, I believe in *hope*. If my stories don't end with happily ever after, I try to ensure that they at least end with hopefully ever after. Sometimes that hope is wrapped up in the next generation, as it was for my parents when they emigrated to Britain from Barbados. Sometimes that hope is interwoven with a flickering belief that better days must surely come. Sam Cooke's song 'A Change Is Gonna Come' still has the power to move me to stillness. If there is any message in my books for young adults, it's that things will get better. It may take time and hard work, but we have to hold onto the belief that things will get better.

Sometimes, when love has flown or is absent, when life knocks us to the ground and won't let us get back up, hope may be all we have left to cling to. I truly believe that, so how would I write stories that say otherwise?

50

Most of the setbacks in my life have propelled me forward. Most of the negative incidents and accidents in my life I have learned to, if not love, then at least appreciate for the unanticipated opportunities and inadvertent benefits they gave me. Each incident and accident has helped to forge the woman I am today. Plus, I have women role models in my family who have taught me the true meaning of resilience, namely my mum and my amazing sister, Wendy.

There have been so many times when I thought my life was ready set to run in one direction, only to find myself heading down a completely different path.

I was told I wouldn't be given a good reference to go to university to read English and Drama with a view to becoming an English teacher because 'Black people don't do that'. Ha! Well, I applied to Goldsmiths College the year after being told that by my careers teacher and I got in. It taught me that if I *really* want something, I shouldn't let anything or anyone stand in my way. The most they can do is slow me down while I find a route around them. The route may be longer in distance and time, but it exists. Mrs T, my careers teacher, slowed me down; she didn't stop me. And I now regard the episode with Mrs T as the dress rehearsal for getting rejection letter after rejection letter when I was trying to find a publisher to take on one of my stories. It made me believe that if one editor said no, surely another editor out there would one day say yes. The incident taught me perseverance and resilience – a life lesson.

When I overheard a doctor tell a nurse at the foot of my bed that I'd be dead before I was thirty, I thought that was it – game over. I did brood on what I'd overheard for quite some time. It took far too long for me to get a grip and treat each day as a blessing, rather than one less day of my life.

And here's the thing.

Overhearing the doctor and nurse turned out to be one of the best things that ever happened to me. It was just the kick up the backside I needed to get out there and do something with my life on my own terms. Something I would find fulfilling and rewarding, otherwise what was the point? When I decided I wanted to be an author for whatever time I had left, I gave up my job and went for it. Would I have become a writer if I hadn't overheard the doctor at the foot of my bed speaking what he thought to be the truth? I wonder. It certainly wouldn't have happened in my twenties. In my case, a time limit served to concentrate my mind and made me get on with living. It made me less afraid to take risks. It also made me appreciate the happy moments to be found in an excellent piece of music, a tasty meal, a hug, a smile, being with loved ones. I wear my favourite perfume whenever I feel like it, not just on special occasions. I dance along the street whenever the mood takes me. (The music video to Jon Batiste's song 'Freedom' is so me!) I think I might've taken those for granted if I hadn't believed I had a time limit. But here's the thing – we all have a time limit. I'm grateful I got to realise that sooner rather than later. It's strange, but there is something breathtaking and exhilarating and dangerous and terrifying about feeling you have nothing to lose. Given a finite amount of time, a use-by date, you're more open to living your best life – at least, that was the case for me. And when I do finally kick the bucket, I'd love for people to remember me, if they remember me at all, with a smile. I'm a firm believer that if you put love out into the world, that's what you get back.

I once lived in a homeless shelter and, though I hated that period of my life, I don't regret it, not any more. Being homeless taught me how to use it up and wear it out. It gave me first-hand knowledge of how too many struggle to get out of the poverty trap. Poverty made me want to take steps to secure a roof over my head, so I bought my own flat when I was twenty-one. I was determined to always be an independent woman with my own money and a room of my own. It took a lot for me to have faith and trust in Neil, my partner (as he was at the time), to be my safety net when I was struggling to get published, but I'm glad I did! Being homeless gave me insight and empathy. That's why I have no time for politicians who tell poor people that if they're struggling it's because they're 'not doing poorness right'. To those who say that if people are having to use food banks, or having to choose between heating or eating, it's because they're not budgeting appropriately, or they don't know how to cook properly, my reply is – fuck off!

I had two miscarriages before I had my daughter, Liz. This just made me appreciate every moment spent with her that much more. And every day I tell her that I love her.

It took me too long to realise that there are some in this world who will see my skin colour and that's all they will ever see. They will think they know everything about me based on my melanin level. I had to learn not to view myself or the world through their eyes. As a child, I used to believe that if I could just sit down and talk to the ones that hated me for my skin colour, then maybe I could persuade them to change their minds. This view persisted well into adulthood. One of the saddest but most liberating days of my life was when I realised that there was absolutely nothing I could say or do, not one single thing, that could stop some from hating me because of my colour – and that's a reflection of them, not me. My best answer to such bigotry would be to move past them and get on with living my best life.

Life poses the question 'why are we here?' I'm still hoping one day to find the answer. In the meantime, I hope to embrace compassion, embrace kindness, and most of all, embrace love. It's the only thing in this world that truly matters.

And I *cough* may have ended a book or two with that exact same refrain.

Because I truly believe it.

51

On 8 February 2022, I reached the prime age of sixty. Sixty years old. Double what I overheard the doctor say that I should expect. Ha! In your face!

Sixty years old . . .
Sixty may be the new forty
    but there are days
        when I feel
            every second
              of
                    my
                          age.

And I love it!

The leg bones creak.
    Lying on my side
    Hurts my knees,
    The right one especially.
    Walking sometimes helps,
    Sometimes it doesn't.
    I like walking
        some days,
    But some days
        it doesn't
            like me.

Going upstairs
The ankles groan.

Going downstairs
          The hips that used to
                    rhythmically shake,
                              Now just ache.

My back
grumbles
if I stand
still
for any length of time.
Sciatica whips
     my legs out
               from under me
                         occasionally.

My middle is taking its time deflating.
     Slimming aids only work
     if you use them.
     Slimming foods only work
     if you eat them
     and nothing else.
     Exercise
     makes me hungry
     Little treats,
     like ice cream
     and dim sum
     and salt and vinegar crisps,
     to celebrate being alive
     and taste buds that work,

slow down the midriff
            deflation
                  process
                        prodigiously.

Eyesight comes and goes.
The eyes become tired
More often.
Vanity
is misdirected energy.
Glasses are a necessity.
Contacts are no longer permanent,
Just now and then,
'Cause who can be arsed?

The hearing goes and comes.
Busy restaurant conversations
No longer work
As they should.
Conversations are littered with
Pardon?
Sorry?
I didn't hear that.
Which sucks mightily.

Frozen shoulders,
Receding gums,
Rough heels and elbows,
Which require more
Not less
Shea butter commiseration,
Cocoa butter consideration,

Moisturiser stimulation,
Supplementary love.

Seats are harder
Beds are lumpier
Sheets are more wrinkly
Faces more crinkly.
Old age
Does not come alone.
Old age
Brings all its friends
To the party
That is my body.
Well, keep them coming
And welcome!
Bring as many
As you like,
Because
It's still better than
the Alternative.

Every day I wake up
And I think,
'I'm still here.'
I open the curtains
And I look out at the sky,
Be it laughter blue,
Misery grey,
Or rage red
Tinged with passionate orange,
And it's always beautiful.
And I think,

'I'm still here.'
I take a shower,
Have some breakfast,
Get to work,
Read emails
Which do my head in,
But I think,
'I'm still here!'
And it's all so much
more Beautiful
Amazing
Invigorating
Exhilarating
Than the Alternative.

So I raise a
glass, and give
a cheer, as I
think to myself,
'I'm still here.'

There you have it.
Some of my life.
Not all of it.
Who has time for that?
But enough of it
For you to get to know a little of me –
As I was,
As I am now,
As maybe one day I might be.
I am so grateful
For all the knockbacks

And the nos
And the doors slammed in my face
Because they've made me –
Hopefully –
Stronger,
Tougher,
More resilient,
More understanding,
Kinder, less naive,
More hopeful,
And the person I am today.
Those knockbacks
And nos
And doors slammed in my face
Have also unfortunately
        made me suspicious
                and wary.
An avid examiner
of a gift-horse's teeth.
Those knockbacks
And nos
And doors slammed in my face
Made me a watcher
As I wait for the other shoe
To descend with force.
An optimistic pessimist?
Or a pessimistic optimist?
Whatever.
The result hasn't always been
Positive,
A +ve
Thumbs up.

But it is what it is.
And what it is,
Is me.

I am a work in progress.
Every day I try to embrace
change and my capacity for it.
Every day I get to rewrite
and retell my life story,
To alter my thinking,
To change my mind,
To grow,
or at least,
to try.
Every day brings love,
And laughter,
And hope.
I am truly blessed
To love and be loved.

When I die,
I've already told
my hubby and daughter
I want them to play
Janet Jackson's 'Together Again'
And Louis Armstrong's
'What a Wonderful World'.
Because the world
This world
Our world
Is so full of *potential*.
And beauty,

And wonder.
And that's what makes
Every day worth living,
Worth loving,
And worth fighting for.
So Neil and Chris, Tara, and Liz,
I love you.
This is me, Malorie,
Signing off.
Peace.

Acknowledgements

For my mum, Ruby, and sister, Wendy, who have shown me by example how to be resilient, tenacious, tough and tender. Much love.

To Aunt Millie and Uncle Everton, who were there when I needed them. Much love.

To my friends, who have put up with my strange behaviours, strange thinking and strange cooking. I'm the world's worst cook but you still don't mind coming for dinner. That right there is true friendship. Much love.

To all the friends I have made since becoming an author who have always had my back, stood at my side, and placed themselves in front of me as a shield when times were rough. I see you. I appreciate you. Much love.

To all the people in publishing who have helped me and my career over the decades, I say a heartfelt thank you. Much love.

And to Lemara and Ana, who worked tirelessly to help me put this autobiography together. You went above and beyond with humour, patience, gentle cajoling and compromise. Thank you for your hard work. I appreciate you. Much love.

And to all my readers – past, present and hopefully future – from the bottom of my heart, thank you for going on my writing journeys with me. You are appreciated. Much love.